Seeking History

Seeking History

Teaching with Primary Sources in Grades 4–6

Monica Edinger

HEINEMANN
Portsmouth, NH

Heinemann
A division of Reed Elsevier Inc.
361 Hanover Street
Portsmouth, NH 03801–3912
www.heinemann.com

Offices and agents throughout the world

The author and publisher wish to thank those who have generously given permission to reprint borrowed material:

Photos of Hester Street from 1904 and 1975 from *New York Then and Now: 83 Manhattan Sites Photographed in the Past and the Present*. Captions by Edward B. Watson. Contemporary photographs by Edmund V. Gillon, Jr. Dover Publications, 1976. Reprinted with permission.

WPA Life Histories are from the Library of Congress, Manuscript Division, WPA Federal Writer's Project Collection.

Detroit Publishing Company Photos are from the Library of Congress, Prints and Photographs Division, Detroit Publishing Company Collection.

Library of Congress Cataloging-in-Publication Data
Edinger, Monica
    Seeking history : teaching with primary sources in grades 4–6 / Monica Edinger.
        p. cm.
    Includes bibliographical references and index.
    ISBN 0-325-00265-7 (alk. paper)
    1. History—Study and teaching (Elementary)—United States. 2. United States—History—Sources. 3. Teaching—United States—Aids and devices. I. Title: Teaching with primary sources in grades 4–6. II. Title.
    LB1582.E37 2000

    372.89′044—dc21

                                                    00-044975

Editor: William Varner
Production: Sonja Chapman
Cover design: Jenny Jensen Greenleaf
Electronic product developer: Eyeon Interactive
Manufacturing: Louise Richardson

Printed in the United States of America on acid-free paper
06 05 04 03 VP 2 3 4 5

Contents

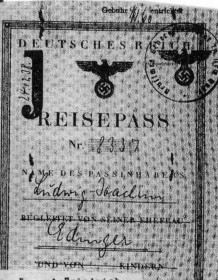

Ich, der unterzeichnete Dr.med.Friedrich
E d i n g e r zu Frankfurt am Main, Gärtnerweg 55,
erkläre hierdurch meine Einwilligung, dass mein
Sohn Ludwig Joachim E d i n g e r geboren am
1.Februar 1922 nach den Vereinigten Staaten von
Amerika auswandert. Ich bemerke ausdrücklich, dass
ich persönlich nicht die Absicht habe, nach Amerika
auszuwandern.

Frankfurt am Main, den 7.Mai 1936.

Dr. med. Friedrich Edinger

Preface

Deutsches Reich Reisepass is printed on the greenish brown cover of the passport I hold in my hand, along with an emblem of an eagle atop a swastika. When I open it up, the first thing that catches my eye is the large red "J" stamped on the upper left-hand corner. The rest of the page is filled with black numbers, places, names—and swastikas. On the next page is my father's photograph at age sixteen surrounded by still more swastikas with the date below: December 24, 1938.

It was my prescient grandmother who saved him. She took him to New York, leaving behind my grandfather, who preferred to stay, convinced that things would get better; he was ultimately deported to Poland and death. Yet despite all I know of my family heritage, I still find it very difficult to believe that something so awful actually happened, that there were real people intent on eliminating a whole ethnic group—mine. The numbers, the information, and the images overwhelm me at times. What helps me are the tangible items, things that I can recognize as real. I sift through them, assemble them in some sort of order, study them, and reorganize them again. I'm a collagist as I try to make meaning, to make sense, to understand my family's harsh history. Photographs of my grandfather. Letters. My father's stories. A Third Reich passport.

The Holocaust is a difficult historical event of which to make sense. It is so horrific, so beyond reason that it is hard to think of as real. If I, whose family was directly affected by the Holocaust, have trouble thinking of it as real, how much more difficult it must be for young Americans who have no such immediate connections to that dreadful time. Certainly there is no lack of teaching material, from Jane Yolen's novel *The Devil's Arithmetic* to Steven Spielberg's film *Schindler's List*. Yet it is the firsthand information that shocks the most: Anne Frank's diary, photographs of Auschwitz, and survivor's oral histories. It is then made unambiguous—

these are true stories of persecution, those are actual images of death. It is this real work with this real stuff that makes the unbelievable real.

Primary sources are real stuff, and real stuff is powerful stuff. Anasazi cliff dwellings in Colorado. Civil War photographs. E. B. White's drafts for *Charlotte's Web*. An heirloom quilt. Birth certificates. All evoke actual past times and events. No matter how well written, no textbook can provide the same sense of being there, of realness, that primary sources provide. They help us in our struggles to make sense of the past. Studying these old things, we all act as historians attempting to unite them for ourselves into coherent and sensible stories of the past. Like artists we use these real things to create collages of historical understanding. They help us as nothing else does to begin to understand the past. This then is a book about using primary sources in the classroom—using these real things to enhance and deepen students' grapplings with history.

I have no memory of my elementary or middle school teachers in the sixties ever using primary sources. My first recollection is of using them in high school, where they were always VERY IMPORTANT DOCUMENTS I can still recite most of the Gettysburg Address and recall tedious explications of the Declaration of Independence, the Constitution, and even the Communist Manifesto. At best they were dull, at worst excruciatingly boring. Certainly they were not something that I considered using when I began teaching. However, over the years my stance has shifted. I've discovered that primary sources are not the boring documents of my own schooling. Indeed, I now consider them just the opposite: one of the most stimulating methods I use to make learning real and powerful for my young students.

For the past thirteen years I have been teaching fourth grade at the Dalton School in New York City. At first I was required to use a textbook for social studies, which I supplemented with various reproducible teacher guides and a handful of trade books. While finding the textbook limited, I was quite content with the blackline masters and the range of trade books written especially for children on the topics I taught. I taught through hands-on projects and probably spent as much time searching for just the right yarn for our Revolutionary War quilt as for information on the actual war.

My awareness of primary sources became heightened when I started teaching a year-long Native American curriculum. Neil Goldberg, an archeologist who had been working with our third graders, and Stephanie Fins, an anthropologist and educator at the American Museum of Natural History, supported me as I began this new curriculum. Native Americans seemed very distant and unreal to my New York fourth graders, and I wanted to change that view. Neil and Stephanie responded by recommending primary sources: reproductions of ancient Anasazi pottery for our unit on the Southwest, potlatch speeches for our studies of the

Northwest Coast, and photographs of ancient cities for our studies of the Maya. This real stuff easily convinced my students that the people they were studying were real too. As a result, I sought out more—folk tales, artifacts, films—whatever would deepen their understanding of indigenous people of the Americas. Poring over a map of the ancient Mayan city of Palenque, touching a Makah transformation mask at the Museum, watching a film of an actual potlatch all stimulated my students in ways I hadn't seen before. Not only did it make everything much more real, but it made my students want to dig deeper—to know more. Before long, whenever I started researching a new topic I began consciously seeking out primary sources.

My transformation was complete the year I began a unit on the Pilgrims. Urged to add a colonial unit to my curriculum, I had been uncertain about how to do so; the colonial unit seemed like such a dull staple of the elementary social studies curriculum. Then one day I met an educator from Plimoth Plantation, who told me all about that remarkable living history museum, a careful recreation of the 1627 settlement. As we talked, my imagination was stimulated. Studying the Pilgrims in depth, I thought, might be just the new angle I needed for that colonial unit. Were there any first-person accounts from the Pilgrims themselves, I asked, especially some that fourth graders could read? But of course, he enthusiastically replied. *Mourt's Relation*, a journal written shortly after the Pilgrims first arrived, would be perfect.

While somewhat dubious that my fourth graders could make any sense out of something published in 1622, much less finding it interesting, I was sufficiently intrigued to visit Plimoth Plantation itself. Once there I was fascinated, and convinced that a focus on the settlement would be just the spark I needed to make a colonial unit new. I read *Mourt's Relation* and discovered it to be a compelling narrative full of wonderful imagery: whales alongside the *Mayflower*, mischievous children, Native American encounters. With a great deal of modeling and support, I tried out some excerpts with my class and was amply rewarded with a level of student understanding and interest that went deeper than any I could have hoped for with secondary sources. I was hooked. There was now no doubt in my mind that primary sources made learning richer and more authentic.

Primary sources now enrich my teaching throughout the day, mostly in our history studies, but with literature as well. My students quickly learn to distinguish primary and secondary sources and become remarkably adapt at interpreting a range of primary sources. Every year my students and I together discover new ways to use this authentic material in learning.

This book is intended to provide upper elementary school teachers with rationales, ideas, and practical ways to use primary sources in their teaching. Traditionally, primary sources tend to be considered difficult, more suitable for high school students than for younger students. Elementary teachers may wonder if their students are ready to make sense of old language, messy documents, and mysterious artifacts. In this book I plan to show that they are. Readers will be able to peek in at my fourth graders as I describe their work with a range of primary sources and how they use them as effectively as more experienced scholars do to interpret the past. My hope is to provide a sufficient mixture of practical and theoretical information to inspire prospective and new teachers as well as experienced ones like myself.

The use of primary sources in teaching and learning, like every other sort of material in the classroom, must be based on theory. In Chapter 1 I will discuss the ideas and theories that underlie my use of these materials in my teaching. I will then describe some of the teaching practices I have used for many years that are particularly effective with primary sources. Although much of my teaching is interdisciplinary and focuses on inquiry and reflection, I've also found primary sources useful in more pragmatic ways as powerful teaching tools for specific content areas and for teaching basic reading, writing, and research skills.

During the summer of 1998, I moderated an Internet bulletin board for educators about primary sources. Especially intriguing were the many different definitions participants offered as to what a primary source actually was. While some of the traditionalists argued that primary sources had to be *significant* firsthand accounts, one teacher took a different stance, insisting that anything *real* was one, even a forest. For others the defining factor was age: one person said that something had to be at least forty years old to qualify. It was a fascinating conversation that helped me to broaden my own ideas about primary sources. In Chapter 2 I will consider definitions of primary sources in more detail and define the term as I use it in this book. The bulk of the chapter will review different kinds of primary sources and provide information on where they might be found.

In teaching we often move from the personal to the wider world. A natural progression often occurs in elementary school: the youngest children focus on family, the middle grades on their local community, and the oldest children on the world. In Chapter 3 I will look at how primary sources can enhance studies from the most personal to the most remote. I will describe how family artifacts can enhance various studies, how a simple neighborhood walking tour can provide a wealth of information, and how to use primary sources to study remote events and places.

From being a teacher who rarely thought about primary sources, I have become one who considers them whenever I design a new unit. In Chapter 4 I will take readers through the creation and revision of a unit I have taught for the past three years that is based completely on primary sources from the Library of Congress's Internet site, American Memory. Why I decided to do this, how I decided what materials to use, how I prepare my students for difficult language and imagery, how I model reading and studying primary sources, how I scaffold the children's experiences, and how I evaluate their learning are some of the issues I will address in this chapter.

In Chapter 5 I will describe a social studies unit I have done for several years on the Constitution, a primary source document that most of us encounter at some point in our schooling. While my memories of this encounter are grim, many of my students consider our Constitution unit their favorite of the year. In part this is due to their pride in tackling a document many would consider beyond them, but it is also because they finish the unit with a sincere appreciation for this living document, a reaction I certainly don't recall when I first struggled through it many years ago. The children learn history, civics, and a remarkable range of critical thinking skills.

While K–12 educators often think of primary sources in terms of social studies, geography, and history, these materials can also enrich literature studies. In Chapter 6 I will discuss the use of primary sources in literature units, particularly in author studies. After reviewing some of the different ways I've used primary sources with literature, I'll describe in detail a special experience my class and I had with Jane Kurtz's novel, *The Storyteller's Beads*. This moving book is based on the actual experiences of Ethiopian Jews immigrating to Israel in the 1980s. We were able to study Jane's writing process through her early drafts of the book and to learn more about Ethiopia itself through artifacts and even a visit to an Ethiopian restaurant.

Every year or so, someone writes yet another article, takes yet another poll, or issues yet another commentary bemoaning our students' lack of knowledge. "They don't know when the Civil War took place!" fusses one. "They know nothing about our government," worries another. "They don't care!" frets still another. "There isn't enough rigor in the curriculum," the pundits announce. Back to basics; to the old days of memorizing facts and taking lots of tests.

Primary sources offer another way to make learning meaningful, creative, and authentic. Viewing, piecing together, and analyzing photographs of Civil War battles to create a history collage will make the facts unforgettable. Connecting Clinton's impeachment with the Constitution will make government come alive. Studying the Holocaust through images, artifacts, and interviews will make evil real. With primary sources our students will care, and care very much indeed.

Acknowledgments

Working as a classroom teacher and writing a book (with a—gasp—CD!) is a foolhardy endeavor. I could never have done it without the help and support of the following people.

My teaching home for many years now has been the Dalton School, and I am grateful to the many people there with whom I've worked: Tom Bonnell, Roxanne Feldman, Stephanie Fins, Jeremy Firstenbaum, Virginia Ford, Neil Goldberg, Sarah Gribetz, Havelock Hewes, Elizabeth Hixson, Stefanie Lerner, Gini Noble, Yolanda Ortiz, Elaine Parisier, Joe Quain, Kris Sternberg, Julia Stokien, and Linda Urmacher. A special thanks goes to Sandy Wang, who assisted me in many tasks, some more interesting than others, to get this book done on schedule. My great appreciation goes to the parents of my students, who have been enormously supportive and appreciative of my work with their children. And most of all, my undying gratitude goes to the children I have been privileged to teach and learn from over the years.

Much of my thinking about teaching with primary sources has been enhanced by my work with the Library of Congress's American Memory Fellows Program. Thank you, Randy Bass, Stanlee Brimberg, Lois Cohn-Klaar, Gail Desler, Leni Donlan, Mike Federspiel, Kathleen Ferenz, Judy Graves, Frances Jacobson, Linda Joseph, Gretchen Sorin, Sonnet Takahisa, Bill Tally, and Susan Veccia.

My intellectual home in cyberspace for years has been the Child_lit list serve. Its members have inspired me, taught me, elevated me, deflated me, and kept me honest. I can't thank them enough for all they have done for me. Special thanks go to Jane Kurtz, who has been such a wonderful and generous online friend, and to Kathy Isaacs, a fellow teacher for life.

I couldn't have done this project without the help and support of the folks at Heinemann: Sonja Chapman, Leigh Peake, and Bill Varner, who conceived this project years ago.

And finally thanks to my family, who complete my history collage: my father, Lewis Edinger; my departed mother, Hanni Blumenfeld Edinger; my sister, Susan Edinger; my niece, Anna; my nephew, Benjamin; and the many other family members who have made me what I am today.

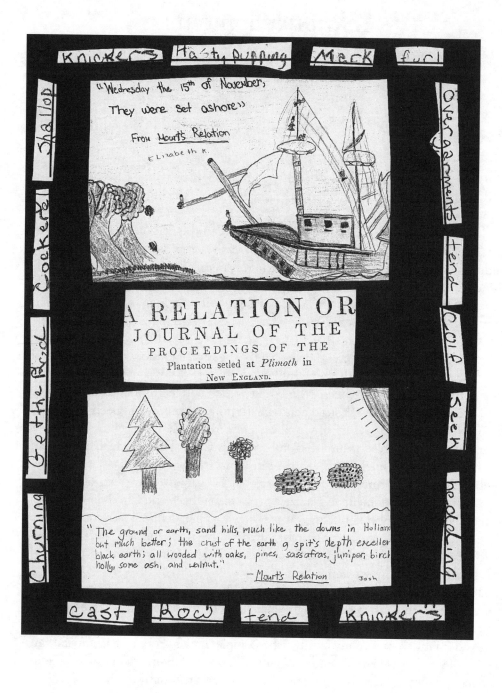

1

Memorable Experiences
Teaching and Learning with Primary Sources

I will remember getting lost on the way to gym.

I will remember our first playstreet and the big fire on Lexington with all the fire engines.

I will remember our first lunch: pizza!

I will remember meeting Sarah for the first time.

I will remember Ms. Edinger reading a story about two cats.

The first day of school is always exhilarating, since it is the start of something, but it is also a challenge and a relief—a challenge for me because there is so much I must do: help my fourth graders feel at home in a new building that includes a high school, establish routines, attach names to faces, and begin to excite these students about all the learning in store, all without also completely overwhelming them; and a relief too, because I need real children around to feel alive as a teacher. For the children too it is a challenge to return to school after a long summer vacation, to find their way around a new building, to reestablish old peer relationships and begin to explore new ones, and to figure out what their new teacher is all about. Yet it is a relief for them as well: all their worries about exactly what the new year would be like are dissipated by being in school at last, a bit nervous and silly perhaps, but ready to begin another year of learning.

   The last day of school is always invariably a bit sad, since it is the end of something; but it too is a challenge and a relief—a challenge because it is hard to plan just the right final activities for a group that has now grown close and learned so much, and a relief because it is June, usually hot, and my students and I are ready for something new and different. At the last moment, just before my students walk out of the classroom for the last time, I bring out an envelope. In it are memory cards, one from each child written at the end of that first day of school. In a quiet circle we begin to reminisce. The children study the memory cards, firsthand

1

records of their feelings on their first day of fourth grade, to see if they can remember what they wrote so many months ago.

When I began teaching, I wanted most of all to create memorable learning experiences for my students. Of my own childhood learning experiences, those I recollected most vividly were projects: putting on plays, creating books, building models. Unfortunately, these didn't happen in school but in our backyard or in our playroom with friends, my sister, or my step-grandmother, a progressive educator. If I hadn't known she was a teacher, it would never have occurred to me that such projects could happen in the classroom; certainly there were none in mine. However, when I became a teacher myself, it was those projects I recollected and brought into my classroom. Remembering those backyard plays, I've helped my students put on plays and other performances. By now I've helped produced hundreds of publications from class literary magazines to individual books. My classes have built models of ancient Mayan cities, created dioramas of historical events, and even, one year, an imaginary island. Over twenty-five years later, my overarching goal remains unchanged: I want my students to have unforgettable learning experiences.

This is a book about teaching with primary sources in upper elementary school. Firsthand materials, I've discovered, can provide students of this age with remarkably rich, engaging, and authentic learning experiences, just the sort of memorable experiences that they won't easily forget. Elementary students are eager learners, even those in the upper grades; they aren't yet unduly preoccupied with the trials and tribulations of teendom and dive into new learning adventures with tremendous pleasure, the more real the better. Unfortunately though, they don't always encounter history in memorable or real ways. The tension we classroom teachers experience between wanting our students to respond emotionally to the past and wanting them to know certain facts about the past often produces lessons that do neither. Our overdependence on secondhand sources, such as textbooks, biographies, and other nonfiction works, can have the unintended effect of making the past seem remote and irrelevant to our students, generating a feeling that the events and people described can't possibly be as real as those in their own lives. Even more problematic is our use of historical fiction to engage children emotionally in studying the past. We may succeed, but often at the expense of children's learning and doing of real history. Primary sources, I find, break down these barriers. They are the real stuff direct from the real past. Whether they stand at the center of a unit or serve as as supplements to the textbook, they are just what elementary students need to see history as real and memorable.

For years I've used primary sources with great success in my fourth-grade classroom to help my students see history not only as real and relevant but as fascinating and intriguing. My students use primary sources to do history. Inquiring about the past, they grapple with the complexities of serious research. Primary sources help my students to think hard about the past and to construct their own views of history instead of relying on the authors of textbooks and tradebooks to do it for them. The result is a classroom of curious, engaged, invested learners, students who are having memorable learning experiences.

A book about my teaching with primary sources also has to be a book about my teaching. There is no way I can discuss how I use primary sources in my classroom without providing the underlying theories, beliefs, and techniques that make me the teacher I am. I moved constantly throughout my childhood, never spending more than three years in the same school until college. It is thus quite amazing to me that I have been teaching at my current school for seventeen years, the past thirteen of them in the fourth grade. A colleague once joked that I would end up like the mother in Alfred Hitchcock's thriller *Psycho*, a skeleton rocking away, still in my very same fourth-grade classroom. Eager to get out of the classroom himself, my former colleague was being a tad sardonic; however, I actually didn't mind the allusion (although I do admit I'd prefer a slightly less macabre image). He was right after all; I'm tremendously content as a fourth-grade teacher. I'm privileged to work in a school that values teachers enormously. We are respected by the administration, by parents, and by our students. How can one not want to teach forever in such a place? I've been fortunate in being able to grow professionally in many ways. Returning from a conference excited about a new idea, I am able to try it out without fear that if it doesn't work, I'll be chastised by someone higher up. I love to read and learn about new ideas, and then decide whether they are truly new or support something unnamed I've already been doing for years. I'm continually learning and growing as a teacher; if I end my life in a rocking chair in my classroom—well, that wouldn't be such a bad memorial for a lifelong teacher, now would it?

My Teaching Goals

Creating memorable learning experiences is not my only goal, although it is one of my most important ones. As a teacher I have many goals. Some of them change little from year to year because they are so fundamental to my educational philosophy. Others come and go because they relate to the needs of a particular class or a particular child. One year, for example, I had a class full of children with serious self-control issues. I spent a great deal of time and energy helping individuals, but my overall teaching goals continued to be academic. Until, that is, we went on a field trip, where the disrespectful behavior was so extreme, that I felt horrified and ashamed. Only then did I realize that my academic goals were useless until these children became responsible and sensitive learners. We returned to school for an emergency class meeting. I told the children of my distress and we established a new goal: to become a respectful and caring community. For the next few months, while my energies were completely directed toward this new goal, the academic ones came second. The children's negative behavior didn't completely disappear (many had profound emotional reasons for their behavior, which needed a great deal more than what I could do in school), but it did improve a great deal. The few weeks when we spent much of our time reflecting on behavior had its effects; a more caring community did evolve and we were able to turn our attention back to academics. Academic and emotional goals together guide me in my work as a teacher.

What follows is an overview of the broad goals that guide me as I plan what goes on in my classroom. This overview is not a finite or conclusive list. Some goals may, in fact, seem a bit vague, and I'm also sure I've left a few out. And no doubt down the road, I'll probably have some new ones. However, these particular goals most closely relate to my use of primary sources in my classroom right now, and where possible I have included specific examples and anecdotes to show that connection.

I Want My Students to Absorb and Retain Significant Information

Historians refer to the *historical record*, by which they mean those dates, names, and other established facts. Although I consider such information important and I am careful to see that my units are rich in content, the content I think is important for my students to know is not necessarily identical to what a fourth-grade teacher in San Francisco thinks is important for her students to know. There is, after all, an awful lot to know in the world. Rather than attempt to stuff as much as possible into my students' heads, I prefer to have them take a close and intensive look at a particular situation and learn as much as they can about that one situation. Instead of learning about the settlement of all thirteen British colonies, for example, my students learn about one settlement, Plimoth, in great detail. They end up knowing remarkable things about the Pilgrims, not simply names, dates, and events. My hope is that the deep investment they make and the pleasure they take in becoming experts about the Pilgrims will cause them to retain enough to use when they revisit the colonial period in eighth grade.

However, others feel differently. In 1987, E. D. Hirsch produced quite a stir with his book *Cultural Literacy*, wherein he argues the case for a discrete set of factual information that every American needs to know. Since then, he has produced a series of books for children outlining this information and spearheaded the "Core Knowledge" movement, which has developed curriculum and started schools in the belief that there is a specific body of knowledge that every literate person must know. Hirsch has been challenged, however, by those who disagree both with his pedagogical approach, which emphasizes breadth over depth, and with his choice of information. His goals are quite laudable, in particular the democratic idea that all children, whatever their background, will have the same information. But I am uncomfortable with the idea that he (and his Core Knowledge colleagues) can be so certain about exactly what children should know, and at a particular age, no less. I am also unconvinced that students will remember facts learned in a superficial way.

The standards movement has also had to deal with the difficult issue of content. The release of the National History Standards in 1994, for example, provoked a tsunami of media reaction, mostly negative. The critics paid little attention to the carefully thought-out pedagogical ideas and made a beeline for the specific informational examples. These, they felt, emphasized social and multicultural history at the expense of traditional political history. As a result, the History Standards were revised and reissued in 1996 with the offending material eliminated. Less contentious were the Curriculum Standards for Social Studies, which avoided too many examples, leaving it to individuals to decide what would be taught. Currently, content is more often suggested in state standards, but these are often so comprehensive, one wonders how on earth the children will manage to absorb and retain it all.

Whatever the disagreement about what and how much should be learned, I have noticed little disagreement about primary sources. In textbooks, state standards, and, even in the Core Knowledge program, primary sources are valued as useful sources of information. These sources acknowledge that the work of historians involves primary sources and that children studying history need the work like historians do.

As I've become more interested in using primary sources in my classroom, I've discovered that they contain much of the information I want my students to learn. For example, we learn about the harvest feast on which Thanksgiving is modeled from *Mourt's Relation*, a firsthand account by the Pilgrims. Studying the early Edison films of Ellis Island helps my students absorb and retain important information about early twentieth-century immigration. And my students are unlikely to forget the Bill of Rights after becoming aware of specific issues in the news related to the first ten amendments. I've noticed that children tend to retain information not for a test, but when they have an investment in learning about it and a genuine desire to learn more. In working with primary sources, my students are learning through genuine inquiry. They want to know more about the Pilgrims, about immigrants, about the Constitution. And because they do, they are far more likely to remember what they have learned long after the unit is over.

I Want My Students to Grapple with Concepts, to Deepen Their Understanding of Complex Ideas and Situations

Governance, war and peace, human rights, and citizenship are the sorts of concepts I have in mind for my students. For many educators, content knowledge is only significant when students grapple with such conceptual understandings. I have long thought in terms of the big, overarching questions that relate to such abstractions when I plan curriculum. For many years the overarching question for my social studies program has been: What is history and who tells it? Because I emphasize primary sources, my students have asked new questions: How can we trust that a primary source is true? What is the difference between a primary and secondary source? Recently I sat down ready to read Barbara Josse's *The Morning Room* to my class, a picture book about a child's immigration from Holland to New York based on Josse's husband's own story. "Is that a primary source?" asked Nick, puzzled, since this book seemed real yet fiction too. After reading the book, the children and I tried to decide. It was classified as fiction, yet it was also based on a true story. Finally we decided it was neither a primary nor secondary source, and thus not not a reliable source of information, but a good story nonetheless.

Many of the examples in this book show students deepening their critical thinking abilities within the study of history. By trying to determine what is true using primary sources, they begin to see that history is not always so certain, that it is a complex area of multiple points of view and multiple interpretations. Figuring out what really happened—or if it is at all possible to determine what really happened—is what real historians do and what my students are beginning to do as well.

I Want My Students to Become Skilled Readers, Writers, and Researchers

Reading primary source texts can be very challenging, but it can also be enormously stimulating and exciting. I love modeling for my students a reading of an old document. In *Far Away and Long Ago* (1998), I described a lesson on reading *Mourt's Relation*, a firsthand account by the Pilgrims published in 1622. I've since done the lesson many times, always in a slightly different way. I always begin by demonstrating how to read an old text. New reading strategies, my students soon note, are needed, since many of their old ones won't work with this kind of text. For example, a current dictionary is not terribly useful because words in 1622 are often used differently and with different meanings than they are today. Better to try context, to read ahead a little, my students decide. Sometimes glossaries from books about the Pilgrims work and Web sites are helpful, but sometimes they aren't. Working together in a group, they learn, is far more effective than trying to

A RELATION OR
JOURNAL OF THE
PROCEEDINGS OF THE
Plantation setled at *Plimoth* in
New England.

Ednesday the sixt of *September*, the Wind comming East North East, a fine small gale, we loosed from *Plimoth*, hauing beene kindly intertained and curteous- ly vsed by diuers friends there dwelling, and after many difficulties in boysterous stormes, at length by Gods prouidence vpon the ninth of *Nouember* follow- ing, by breake of the day we espied land which we deemed to be *Cape Cod*, and so afterward it proued. And the appearance of it much comforted vs, especially, seeing so goodly a Land, and woodded to the brinke of the sea, it caused vs to reioyce together, and praise God that had giuen vs once againe to see land. And thus wee made our course South South West, purposing to goe to a Riuer ten leagues to the South of the Cape, but at night the winde being contrary, we put round againe for the Bay of *Cape Cod ;* and vpon the 11th. of *Nouember*, we came to an anchor in the Bay, which is a good harbour and pleasant Bay, circled round, except in the entrance, which is about foure miles ouer from land to land, compassed about to the very Sea with Okes, Pines, Iuniper, Sassafras, and other sweet wood ; it is a harbour wherein 1000. saile of Ships may safely ride : there we relieued our selues with wood and water, and refreshed our people, while our shallop
was

Figure 1–1. Mourt's Relation

7

work alone. These are new skills I have to teach my students in order for them to make meaning out of a seventeenth-century text. For American Memory, the Library of Congress Web site of primary sources that we use in our immigration studies, they need still other specialized skills: how to make sense of bibliographical data, how to skim through long oral history transcripts to find what they want, how to look carefully at images, as well as how to use a search engine efficiently, and how to save files. All these skills need to be explicitly taught so that the students can use the primary sources effectively.

Writing is continually happening in my classroom so there are many writing activities in this book. Primary sources are amazing materials for teaching and learning writing skills. Certainly they can provoke children's imagination and spur their creativity, but they can also be useful in more practical ways such as spelling. My students never fail to be delighted when they learn that "Plymouth" and "Plimoth" are both acceptable spellings, not to mention "Plymoth," because spelling was unstandardized in 1622. These three spellings would have been equally acceptable and maybe a few more as well. It is great fun to look at a reproduction of *Mourt's Relation* (see Figure 1–1, p. 7) with its original spelling intact (it was edited by George B. Cheever and published in 1848 as *The Journal of the Pilgrims at Plymouth in New England, in 1620: Reprinted from the Original Volume*) full of such nonstandardized spelling. It is especially reassuring for those of us who are dreadful spellers! The first year of the Pilgrim unit I started a Pilgrim vocabulary chart. On it went especially interesting words we came across in our readings, words we wanted to learn more about, words that sounded wonderful and strange, and words that the children wanted to use in their own stories. Noticing, that first year, how intrigued the children were by these words, the following year I developed a homework assignment: create a Pilgrim glossary (see Figure 1–2, p. 9). I asked each child to choose ten nouns, ten verbs, and ten other parts of speech (adjectives, adverbs, and so on) from their Pilgrim materials (which were mostly firsthand accounts) and define them as best they could. The next day we had a grand time creating several class glossary charts. I had intended to spend one period on this, but the children had so many words and were so engaged, we ended up spending three periods completing the charts. The assignment turned into a unique grammar lesson as we struggled to figure out what part of speech many of these old, obsolete words were. In subsequent years I've done this activity again and then required the children to use words from the glossary in their own stories and to add glossaries at the end, along with the usual bibliographies.

Research skills are at the heart of most upper elementary social studies programs. And since I've always loved research, I've always made sure I include a research project in my teaching. However, the specific methods and approaches have changed a great deal since I began teaching in the 1970s. Then, my research

Name: **Sarah W**　　　　　　　　Date:_____

Personal Pilgrim Glossary

NOUNS

WORD	MEANING
Shallop	Large boat
gale	small gust of wind
habitation	living Place
Kine	cow
draught	some medicine
poppet	doll
notion	a thought (idea)
tale	story
sassafras	a kind of tree
venison	deer meat
elder	older person
feathered men	Native Americans
pallet	a straw filled bed

VERBS

WORD	MEANING
cast	throw-up
scour	to have diarrhea
unship	unload
befell	happened
felling timber	cutting down trees
giveth	to gives
dose	to give medicine
trashed	to hurt
bestow	to give
dwell	to live
felling	chopping
thrash	to hurt

Figure 1–2. Sarah's Pilgrim Glossary

9

projects were creative, but the structure was rigidly set. I would decide on a topic, find the materials, set up the structure, and oversee the project step-by-step. A big change for me was learning about the writing process approach (Graves, 1983). I stopped insisting kids work through the project in one set way. Instead, I encouraged them to discover their own best ways of doing research. For example, rather than insisting that children complete an outline and notecards to my specifications, I would do minilessons in which we considered different planning techniques (including, but not limited to outlines) and different note-taking techniques (including, but not limited to notecards). Another change occurred as I began to refocus my social studies program so that the children were working and thinking as historians. Now my students do far more of the initial work, figuring out good research questions, how best to take notes, and what they really want to know. Of course, my job isn't easier, just different. Now I have to model ways of doing research, to structure my students' evolving research skills development, and be there for them as they take steps to do it on their own.

I continue to provide direct instruction on various research skills along with ample opportunities for my students to practice what I've modeled in doing their own research. While basic research skills—developing good research questions, planning, note taking, drafting and revising a product (written or done in some other media), providing an author's note in the case of historical fiction, and understanding and creating bibliographies and glossaries—continue to be important, I've had to add a significant new element: online research. The Internet offers a wealth of material, but it also requires a great deal of skill in using search engines efficiently and in evaluating resources.

I Want My Students to Be Creative

I have always enjoyed artistic projects. I've done them on my own all my life and in my classroom. Dance, theatrical performances, publications, and visual art are part of my teaching every year. For many years I associated the word *creative* only with artistic endeavors such as these, but now my thinking has shifted, primarily due to Howard Gardner (1985) and his theory of multiple intelligences. While I had always delighted in children's remarkable and original thoughts in our various studies, I would probably not have considered them "creative" in the "artistic creation" sense until I discovered Gardner's ideas. He helped me rethink my concept of creativity to encompass a range of disciplines and life behaviors. I now can appreciate the child who is creative in solving a playground dispute as well as one who produces a lovely drawing. Creativity, I now realize, comes in many shapes and forms. And here, primary sources factor in as well. Throughout this book I will include examples in which primary sources are used in creative ways: some are creative projects inspired by primary sources while others are creative projects using primary sources.

I Want My Students to Come up with Wonderful Ideas

I start the year with a close study of E. B. White's *Charlotte's Web*. One of the reasons I do so is because the children already know and love the book and enjoy digging more deeply into it in a new and different way. I also do it because E. B. White is one of the most amazing writers of all time. We use many primary sources in this study: White's many drafts and notes for the book, photographs of his farm, and letters he wrote about the book. Once the children have done a first reading (or, more likely, a rereading) of the book I model a close reading of the first chapter for them. (For more about this unit please see the E. B. White chapter in Edinger [1995], *Fantasy Literature in the Elementary Classroom.*) Embedded in this modeling are introductions to literary devices such as irony and foreshadowing. Each child then takes on a chapter to study in a similar fashion. When it comes time to present these chapters, I move the desks into a configuration as close to a college seminar table as is possible, and each child presents his or her discoveries to the group. And year after year, I am awestruck by what these children tease out of the text. My favorite for many years was a child's observation that Charlotte's death occurs not only in the middle of the fairground but in the middle of a beautifully written paragraph.

As exciting as it is when a child comes up with a truly original idea, I do not expect most of my students' ideas to be original. Their thinking about fairy tales, developed after a deep and rich study of one classic tale, "Cinderella," would not be new to many, but they *are* new to my students, and that is what matters to me. Constructing their own ideas, whether they are new to the world or not, is the most important thing.

I Want My Students to Produce Works of Art

While I now recognize that creativity is not just about art, I am still very interested in my students' artistic expression. Since I have always enjoyed artistic projects, I encourage my students in similar endeavors. Many of the classroom activities described in this book will involve some sort of artistic final product, such as a book, Web page, collage, model, or performance, and I have found primary sources invaluable in helping my students create these works. Looking at primary sources helps my students think through their own plans, although there was a time when I worried that showing them such examples might constrict their own efforts. I've since discovered that this is not the case. Instead, they use primary sources to guide them in their own work. I enjoy seeing them use work my former students have done as a sort of primary source. During last year's Pilgrim study, for example, my students relied on former students' books as models as they began to consider how to publish their own.

I Want My Students to Develop Self-Awareness

A significant achievement of human life is gaining a sense of self. Our American heritage is one that very much values the individual. Many educational theories are related to the idea of self-discovery. Those of us who adhere to Howard Gardner's theory of multiple intelligences, for example, are careful to provide a variety of educational experiences to accommodate these different intelligences and to encourage children to discover their own particular strengths. Child-centered activists like Alfie Kohn (1999) advocate a curriculum that is generated by children rather than by adults. Knowing one's own interests and passions is critical to such an approach.

In his groundbreaking book *Emotional Intelligence*, Daniel Goleman (1995) describes self-awareness as "the sense of an ongoing attention to one's internal states. In this self-reflexive awareness mind observes and investigates experience itself, including the emotions" (p. 46). One of the ways I helped my unruly class (the year of the horrible field trip) was to ask the children to reflect continually on their own behavior. Their constant self-evaluation was effective. The children were able to behave more appropriately because they were monitoring themselves, not waiting for me or another adult to let them know what was appropriate. Such reflection also enables children to begin to realize their own particular tastes and learning styles. For example, there are many ways to write, and I want to make my students aware of different techniques in order to discover which one works best for them. I write best by simply writing and rewriting. Somehow I work through my ideas best in prose. Others however, are able to think through their idea before putting words down. And when they do, very little revision is necessary. Still others benefit from lengthy outlines. Figuring out one's own writing style is the sort of self-awareness I want my students to develop.

I Want My Students to Be Empathetic Human Beings

Empathy is the ability to understand someone else's situation, to "walk in someone else's shoes." It leads, according to Goleman, "to caring, altruism, and compassion. Seeing things from another's perspective breaks down biased stereotypes, and so breeds tolerance and acceptance of differences" (p. 285). One of my most fervent goals is to help my students be able to connect with others, especially to those different from themselves. I am certainly delighted when my students demonstrate a solid knowledge of facts about the Pilgrims, are able to explain the importance of religious freedom, and produce wonderful works of historical fiction about the Mayflower journey, all through deep engagement with original materials. However, most important of all is whether they have connected emotionally to these people of long ago. Can my students imagine themselves in such a situation? Can they relate the experience of the Pilgrims to that of other immigrants who have also had to flee their homeland because of religious persecution? This sort of empathetic understanding is critical to my work as a teacher, and I have discovered that primary sources are very successful in bringing my students to such understanding. There is something quite extraordinary about reading the words of those long-ago *Mayflower* passengers, something that resonates and helps my students connect with them emotionally.

My Practice

My goals would be meaningless if I did not attempt to achieve them in practice. Over the years I've discovered several particularly effective methods for reaching my goals. The following methods are by no means the only ones I use, but these are fundamental to my teaching and have been especially effective in my work with primary sources.

Letters

I began corresponding with my students after reading Nancie Atwell's wonderful book, *In the Middle* (1998). I loved the way she was able to engage in a private conversation with each child about his or her reading. The first year I tried it, however, I was overwhelmed. My biggest mistake was having the children write to me daily. They enjoyed doing so and took longer and longer each day, until little time remained for other activities. And the more they wrote, the more I felt I needed to write back, with the result that I spent hours responding after school. My second mistake was allowing them carte blanche to write whatever they wanted about their reading. I provided them with suggestions, but, believing in the importance of ownership, did not insist on any particular topic. Some students had no problem writing about intriguing aspects of the text. Many others, however, simply wrote retelling their reading of the night before. This, I realized, was what was taking so much class time. And coming up with a sincere response became more and more difficult. What could I possibly write after yet another three pages recapping the latest escapades of the Sweet Valley Twins? The following year I made journal writing a weekly activity.

I've experimented with letter writing journals over the years and discovered effective ways to use them, especially in achieving many of my learning goals. In letters to me, my students have reflected on difficult and complex issues in literature and in our historical studies. Some have found these letters the best vehicle for understanding. Others simply approach their letters in creative ways, by writing poems about books and ideas. One reason these journals have become such effective learning devices is that I'm more demanding of my students. They may write only once a week, so what they write is far more thoughtful than a retelling of their reading. I often ask them to write on a specific issue: Who is the hero of *Charlotte's Web*? Do you think Olaudah Equiano (a former slave whose autobiography I read aloud) would want to go back to Africa? Do you think the film *The Long Long Journey* (about a Polish immigrant to New York) was based on a true story? These sorts of provocative questions arise in our class discussions and inspire the children to think more deeply.

Since my students are so familiar with letter writing, they very much enjoy reading letters by the authors they study; E. B. White and Lewis Carroll, in particular, are masters of the form. Letters are also important primary sources in our immigration and Pilgrim studies.

But best of all are occasions to write to individuals outside the school. In 1997, for example, I read a *New York Times* article to my students about a controversial exhibit at the Ellis Island Immigration Museum on the killing of Armenians by Turks early in the twentieth century. The problem arose when Museum officials asked the exhibit's organizers to remove fifteen photographs that they felt were too gory for the many children who visited the museum. Having just visited Ellis Island themselves a few days earlier, my students had strong feelings about the issue, and I suggested that we write a letter to the editor.

October 15, 1997

To the Editor:

Somini Sengupta in the October 14th news article, "Ellis Island, Yielding, Permits Photos of Armenian Massacre" writes that Ellis Island "museum officials considered the photos inappropriate for a place visited by hundreds and thousands of young school children every year." As some of these young school children who recently visited the Museum we disagree with this. We feel that the whole story should be told even if parts of it are unpleasant. We think all fifteen photographs should be shown with a sign warning visitors of their harsh content. Some of us feel we would have gone to see the photographs while others of us wouldn't have. Yet all of us agree they should be shown.

Sincerely,
Ms. Edinger's Fourth Grade
The Dalton School

I emailed the letter and was very excited the next day to get a call from the *New York Times*. They might publish it, I was told. The *Times* person and I worked on shortening the letter, and then she dropped a bombshell: I had to select two children from the class as the letter's authors. But it wasn't two children, it was truly the whole class, I told her. That may be, she responded, but they couldn't publish it that way. With mixed feelings I went to my students. I explained the situation to them and they agreed to have two names randomly selected as authors. We then watched avidly to see if the *Times* would publish the letter, but they never did. It was my students' first experience with the vagaries of real-world publishing. However, the experience of writing a letter and receiving a response resonated nonetheless.

A month later we again wrote a class letter, this time to Gail Carson Levine, author of *Ella Enchanted,* a book I had read aloud. I thought that Levine, a first-time author, might enjoy a letter from a class of fans. We carefully drafted a letter and were thrilled when we received not only a return letter, but an offer to visit as well!

Letters have become more and more central to my teaching. Starting with letters in journals I've moved on to consider correspondence in a range of learning situations. Many of our letter exchanges happen over the Internet. (In Chapter 6 I will describe at length a letter-writing project that came about because of the Internet.) Yet even as I use email and other forms of electronic communication, I continue to use old-fashioned stationery as well. Either way, the letters function as opportunities for my students to write about primary sources and to write their own primary sources.

Portfolios

Those of us who are committed to a process approach to writing instruction are vigilant about asking students to keep all drafts of their work to illustrate their process as writers. I tell them over and over that these artifacts show as much about them as learners as their final published pieces. All year long my students collect their writing and other artifacts of their learning. Periodically they look through these portfolios as they assess their growth as learners, and they are often surprised at how they've grown in a few short weeks or months.

My students maintain working portfolios throughout the school year. During a unit, they keep all their work (writing drafts, sketches, notes, etc.) in a folder. At the end of the unit I ask them to organize all this work according to an order of their own choosing, complete a self-evaluation about their learning for the unit, clip it all together, and put it into their working portfolios. Smaller projects and other work go into these portfolios as well. Then, at the end of the year, I ask each child to create a presentation portfolio. I show them some of my art portfolios as well as some presentation portfolios done by former students. These presentation portfolios are going to be their fourth grade memoirs, the original records of their work for the year. The children bring in binders with acetate sleeves to hold their work and then spend several days going through their working portfolios determining what they want to keep and how they want to organize it. Once the presentation portfolios are completed, we have an exhibition for parents in which they are prominently featured. The best part of all, though, is the following September, when many former students lend me their portfolios. I use them throughout the school year to show my current students how students from the previous year approached different projects. These presentation portfolios, full of learning about primary sources, then become primary sources themselves.

Charts

When I teach, I use charts constantly. However, unlike many teachers I don't have an easel. I prefer to create a chart with my students and then post it somewhere in the room to give us all a firsthand view of the learning that has taken place. These charts can be drafts of a class story, a list of rules about how to use paragraphs, or a list of what we know about something. At the start of the year my classroom is completely bare, but as the year goes on the walls fill up with these charts. Some years ago I came across Post-it chart paper, and now I can stick my charts up everywhere! So now they appear on window shades, high up near the ceiling, and wherever I can find an empty space not already occupied by other samples of student learning. Not only do I keep the charts up all year, but I save them. I find them incredibly helpful when planning. Looking at the charts from previous years help me recollect exactly what I did. Charts, a common and often taken-for-granted teaching technique, are wonderful primary sources and wonderful when teaching with primary sources.

A good example is our Hurricane Floyd chart. Weather scares New Yorkers. Meteorological events that other communities seem to handle with aplomb become big events in the Big Apple. Hurricane Floyd was due to rip through the New York metropolitan area on September 17, 1999. In fearful anticipation, schools were closed, and people left work early resulting in snarled traffic and misery. Fortunately, New York City was spared the worst, and damage was minimal. The experience of the residents of the nearby suburbs in New Jersey and New York State was far worse. Several days later, many were still without power or phone service and trying to deal with serious flooding. Upon our return to school I pointed out to my students that since they had witnessed a historic storm, their firsthand accounts were a sort of primary source.

I showed them the front page of the *New York Times* and commented on the modest size of the headline "Disruption but Limited Damage in Lashing From Waning Storm," not nearly as large, I noted, as the headline on the day Clinton was impeached. Next, I read to them a feature article by N. R. Kleinfield, "Storm Hits a City That Had Mostly Left Town," which included the line, "It was a particularly great day to be a kid. No school and yet your apartment didn't collapse." I then asked the children to provide their eyewitness accounts of the storm for a chart. The chart is still up, months later, a primary source full of eyewitness accounts of Hurricane Floyd:

Hurricane Floyd

MICHELE: Worst birthday I ever had because I couldn't go outside.

JONATHAN: The storm caused a lot of traffic problems.

ALEX: My backyard was flooded for the 2nd time this summer.

NICOLAI: The sewer was overflowing at my house.

MORGAN: There is a big mud river in Central Park.

JOSH: There was so much rain I couldn't see out my window.

MATTHEW: Outside my apartment there was about an inch of water. You could skip rocks.

DANIELLE: It would pour again and then stop, pour again and then stop.

NATHANIEL: A lot of people had greater expectations [than what really happened].

ELIZABETH K.: There were rivers in the gutters.

CHELSEA: Even leaving work early my dad got home at nine o'clock.

NICK: Walking three blocks to my friend's house my shoes got filled with water.

MS. E: The next morning while running in Central Park I saw tree branches everywhere.

REBECCA: So foggy you couldn't see out the window.

Publishing

I am a bookophile. I admit it. Since beginning as a teacher, I have had publishing projects of one sort or another going on in my classroom every year. I still have books my classes made over twenty years ago, books full of photographs of children long grown-up and their writings. Now they are primary sources for my work as a teacher. Some years ago I developed a newspaper unit. After several weeks of studying the daily *New York Times*, my students each created an individual family newspaper. (This project was so long ago, that the copies I still have are mimeographed, not photocopied!) They are wonderful sources of life ten years ago. Another publishing project I did with students for years involved memoirs. The children wrote them and made two books out of them—one to take home and one for the class library. In subsequent years, those extra copies—these primary sources—were much in demand during our independent reading period. More recently, my students have created picture books from oral history interviews with immigrants and written historical fiction about the Pilgrims. With the Internet, we've also done publishing projects: after studying *Alice's Adventures in Wonderland* we created a complete illustrated edition of our own on the Web. Another class's "found poems" were published on the Web. There is something about publishing that I love, and throughout this book there will be plenty of examples of classroom publishing activities.

Read Alouds

Since I love books, I also love sharing them with children. At the end of the day I have a read-aloud time. I turn the overhead lights off and the small lamp next to my special wingback chair on. The children get pillows and find comfortable places: on the rug, on or under a desk, wherever they wish. Then I begin to read. During this read-aloud time I always read fiction, a chapter or two a day from a book I know my class will enjoy. But I read aloud at other times too. At the end of our morning meeting I will read an article from the newspaper, a picture book in connection with our various history and social studies units, or even a letter sent to me that might be of interest to my students. Often these read alouds are from primary sources: a letter Lewis Carroll wrote to a child friend or William Bradford's memoir, in which he mentions "pilgrims," which is how those Mayflower passengers became known as Pilgrims. Recently, a young assistant teacher, new to our school, commented that one especially important thing that she had learned while working with us in the fourth grade was the value of reading aloud. She had previously worked with younger children and had assumed fourth graders were too old for this. Watching me read aloud primary sources, picture books, informational books, and other nonfiction was a revelation for her.

I've been teaching fourth grade for some time now, but I used to teach fifth and sixth grade as well. And I read aloud to those age groups too. I find reading aloud a wonderful way to develop community and to provide information in a different way. And primary sources that may seem to challenging for students to read independently may well be perfectly understandable to them when read aloud.

Questions & Answers

Q: How about context? Isn't it pretty hard for kids to make sense of something like *Mourt's Relation* without knowing something about the Pilgrims first?

A: Absolutely. Context is critical. Before my students tackle *Mourt's Relation* they have already done a great deal of secondary source reading about the Pilgrims. They have that background in place as they wade into this strange seventeenth-century text. Without that background it would be exhausting and futile. I'm sure, in fact, I would get outright rebellion before long. However, with a strong background, they love tackling the document and even tell me it wasn't that hard to read!

However, I can't tell you exactly how much context to provide. It depends on the particular primary source, the time period, the age group, the particular group of students and their needs, and your own teaching style. How much context or background is needed is something only you, the teacher, can determine. I would, however, warn you not to overdo it. It is tempting for those of us who love history to get carried away and take our students farther than they can go. While my nine-year-olds can read and understand very old texts, I only ask them to read a few pages, not a whole book. Nor do I get completely frustrated when, despite all my efforts, a child persists in responding to an old text through contemporary eyes, as in, "Euww, where did they go to the bathroom on the *Mayflower?*" I'm realistic about their abilities, yet I also want them to have an appropriate amount of background to use *Mourt's Relation* effectively to achieve the learning goals I have for them.

Q: What sort of preparations do you make before using a primary source with your students?

A: As I mentioned above, I do not ask my students to read all of *Mourt's Relation*. I give them a packet that consists of a few excerpts I've carefully selected. One is a letter with the only known description of the first Thanksgiving. Others describe the *Mayflower* journey, first meeting Indians, and other situations that I feel will interest them. To make the reading easier I enlarge the pages when I photocopy them. Additionally, I do several lessons modeling how to read the material before sending them off in groups to read it together. I begin our work with the American Memory Web site in the same way, by modeling how to do an online search, how to makes sense of the bibliographic records, how to analyze an early film to decide if it serves your needs or not. Preparing the primary sources themselves, as I did with *Mourt's Relation*, is key in working with elementary students. Without altering the material itself, you can make it more legible and easier for children to make sense of. Additionally, plenty of modeling is critical. Time and again I have seen my students remind one another of a technique they observed me do first. Finally, I recommend many visual aids: handouts, charts, and other such materials to support children in their inquiry with primary sources.

Q: Okay, I'm hooked. But where do you find all these amazing resources?

A: I've been doing this for a while now. In later chapters I'll give more specific information about finding primary sources. Once I've decided a topic, I have great fun seeking out primary sources. Museum educators, in particular, are very enthusiastic and eager to help. Those at Plimoth Plantation have given me many useful suggestions. I make a point of always checking out museum shops and have found great stuff that way. When I taught the Maya, one of my favorite primary sources was a reproduction of a piece of Mayan pottery I found in a market. I've found stuff on the Internet and even on the street! (I have a wonderful old Underwood typewriter discovered on the street many years ago. More recently, while running, I saw the coolest old cash register, but it was simply too heavy for me and I most reluctantly left it behind for someone else.) I'm constantly clipping and saving news articles that may be of use one day. I've also gotten lots from parents, kids, and colleagues. Once people know you're on the lookout for stuff, they will bring it to you!

2

The Never-ending Journey
Defining Primary Sources

A primary source is when you see or read the actual thing.

The definition of a primary source is a source that is original, has not been changed at all.

Something that comes straight from the truth.

I think that a primary source is the first account where first encountered and first recorded.

I have always loved history. As an undergraduate I almost majored in the subject. One of my favorite aspects of the discipline was doing research: tussling with the difficult language of an obscure medieval treatise, tracking down a rare source, and acquiring lots of information on a topic—I simply loved doing this; card catalogues, library stacks, rare book rooms—all favorite places for me. And then to make sense of it all: to compare one account with another, to consider how other factual information figured in, and eventually to use it all to come to an understanding of a historical event—all great stuff, I thought. Standing in a kiva at Mesa Verde, Colorado, made me feel that I might begin to gain a sense of the Anasazi and why they deserted their cliff dwellings. I was sure I could visualize Lewis Carroll telling his tales to Alice as I visited his old haunts in Oxford.

Through my historical research in college, my travels, and later as I began developing curriculum for my elementary students, I didn't think much about the definitions of primary and secondary sources. If anyone had asked me, I would have said it was obvious. Textbooks, the *World Book Encyclopedia* with its wonderful color inserts, a book about medieval architecture—secondary sources, or so I thought; The Constitution, Da Vinci's sketches, the Temple of the Moon outside Mexico City—primary sources, or so I thought. Secondary sources were interpretations of firsthand material. Primary sources were the undoctored originals. The differences between them, between textbooks and documents, between biographies and diaries, seemed so certain, it was not even worth thinking about.

As my teaching evolved to a point where authentic activities and materials became more important to me, these certainties began to erode. Wanting the children to work as literary and historical scholars, I moved away from secondary materials as the main source of information and sought out primary sources—and I discovered that it was much more complicated than I used to think. Again and again what I thought was true turned out not to be. I learned that the original Mayflower Compact has disappeared; my so-called "original facsimile" was actually cobbled together from a copy of the text and a list of the signatures from somewhere else. There was the revelation that my much beloved edition of Anne Frank's diary had been significantly edited by her father in order to present her in a particular light. And the kiva at Mesa Verde was largely a restoration. So how "original" were any of them? As for secondary sources, these became difficult too. Weren't all textbooks secondary sources? If so, what was I to make of that nineteenth-century geography textbook I picked up in a used book store. The information therein was completely out-of-date and often racist to boot. Indeed, a secondary source when new, it was now a primary source, revealing pedagogical attitudes at the time it was written. I became uncomfortable. I had put up student-created charts in my classroom with lists of what primary and secondary sources were. My students wanted firm distinctions and so did I. But was that possible?

I decided to return to my favorite activity: research. Others were likely to have struggled with this problem and resolved it. With their help, I was sure I could resolve this dilemma and come up with some solid way of distinguishing between these two types of sources.

I began by investigating what two other history educators thought. In her book about teaching history, *Connecting with the Past,* Cynthia Stokes Brown defined primary sources "as any material created at the time of an event, or later from the memory, by someone in the event" (1994, p. 17), while David Kobrin, a professor at Brown University, wrote in *Beyond the Textbook*: "When teaching, I define primary sources broadly to include any documents, written materials, or artifacts that were created contemporaneous to the events they describe" (1996, p. 13). These two definitions, partly in agreement and partly not, typified my difficulty in creating an absolute definition. Both Brown and Kobrin considered material created at the time of an event a primary source, but Brown went a bit further by also including memoirs. But were memoirs reliable? So many seemed fictionalized. Could I really consider them primary sources as Brown did?

Turning to the Internet, I came across the library at the University of California, Berkeley, which defined primary sources as: "the evidence left behind by participants or observers" (<www.lib.berkeley.edu>) I liked the word *evidence* and the acknowledgment of the creators of the primary sources. Next, I discovered the Primary Sources Research section of the Yale University Library. I was delighted with their definition: "A primary source is firsthand testimony or direct evidence concerning a topic under investigation. The nature and value of a source cannot be determined without reference to the topic and questions it is meant to answer. The same document, or other piece of evidence, may be a primary source in one investigation and secondary in another. The search for primary sources does not, therefore, include or exclude any category of records or documents." (<www.library.yale.edu/ref/err/primsrcs.htm>) I liked this definition because it made clear how slippery the identification process is. Like the University of California, Berkeley library staff, the people at Yale used the word *evidence* and suggested the creators of this evidence by using the word *testimony*. Without projecting a boundless world, this definition leaves wide open the possibility that a range of materials may be considered primary sources, depending on the particular investigation.

Original sources, firsthand accounts, evidence, documents, records, information, testament, narrative, left behind—these words and phrases all rolled around in my mind as I attempted to synthesize what I had read, observed, discussed, and considered to date about primary and secondary sources. Finally I concluded that I could never come up with absolute definitions. New information, further conversation and reflection, and more experience with children would certainly affect my ideas and cause me to revise them.

Here are my current working definitions of these slippery, ever-changing terms.

> *Primary source*: Any material created by a person, including firsthand accounts of particular events.
> *Secondary source*: Any interpretation of a primary source.

Types of Primary Sources

As difficult as it was to come up with workable definitions of primary and secondary sources, another quandary immediately presented itself: how to create a helpful list of different kinds of primary sources. I have managed to do so, but my list is both idiosyncratic and incomplete: idiosyncratic because I have my own very particular and still evolving ideas of what are primary sources are; incomplete because there is simply no way for me to know or adequately research every possible sort of primary source in existence. For now, I've divided primary sources into five categories: text, audio material, objects, visual material, and places.

Text

Published and Printed Material I'm a bibliophile and can happily spend hours browsing in a used bookstore, especially if there is a good assortment of children's books. Books are fascinating primary sources. I have the first book I ever remember reading on my own as well as all those amazing books of my grandmothers'. Newspapers and magazines also offer wonderful views into the past. I have the *Life* magazine published after President Kennedy's death as well as the *New York Times* from the day of President Clinton's reelection. Catalogues, which come to my mailbox fast and furious, are another source of historical information. Even flyers, such as the never-ending Chinese take-out menus we New Yorkers find in our lobbies every day, offer a particular view of the past.

Manuscripts Manuscripts can be handwritten, typed, or even word processed. What distinguishes them from the previous category is that they are unpublished. I love looking at the early drafts of well-known books. A delight is E. B. White and Peter Neumeyer's *The Annotated Charlotte's Web*, which includes, in an appendix, several of White's early drafts of his classic children's book. For Constitution scholars, there are multiple drafts of that famous document available for study.

Letters Letters are another amazing source of information. I still recall writing weekly letters to my grandparents because long-distant telephoning was too expensive for my family. Earlier generations were far more prolific correspondents. Before the telephone, mail was delivered several times a day, and it wasn't unusual for individuals to write each other more than once in the course of a single day. Serious letter-writers kept track of their correspondence in ledgers and kept copies in letterbooks. I was honored recently to see one of George Washington's letterbooks at the Library of Congress.

Diaries and Journals Diaries and journals are incredibly moving but complicated primary sources. After all, they weren't usually written for others to see. I still have the diary I kept in my twelfth year, although I cannot bear to read more than a page or two, still humiliated by the trials of early adolescence I know are there. It was given to me by my grandmother along with *The Diary of Anne Frank*, in 1964, shortly before we embarked on a year-long sojourn in Europe. During that year we visited the recently opened Anne Frank House in Amsterdam, where a small display case housed Anne's diary. I noticed that it was almost identical to mine, with the same plaid cloth cover and lock, and I now assume that my grandmother brought it with her in 1936 when she left Frankfurt, where the Franks had also lived. For many, Anne's diary is a touchstone primary source for the Holocaust. Other diaries and journals, while not necessarily as deeply moving as Anne's, nonetheless offer unparalleled perspectives on the past.

Documents My dictionary defines a document as "a written or printed paper furnishing information or evidence, a legal or official paper." This, in my view, could include those very important documents I have referred to already (such as the Constitution) as well as smaller documents: a birth certificate, for example, or a diploma, or a will.

Records By records, I mean information such as census and weather data. In 1998 I attended the Kids Learning History II Conference at the Smithsonian in Washington, D.C. During one session, Lynda Kennedy, educational coordinator of the Lower East Side Tenement Museum, gave participants one page of a 1914 attendance book from a public school in New York. Just the range of names, scratched over birthdays, and changes of address told us a lot. During our Pilgrim unit, my students find the inventories of individual Mayflower passengers quite useful because they give us a sense of what these people considered important enough to bring to the New World.

Audio

Speeches There is something thrilling, I think, in hearing certain historical figures speak. Very few American children make it through elementary school, for example, without hearing one of Martin Luther King's speeches. The first president I was really aware of was John F. Kennedy, and my mother was from Berlin so I am always captivated by his "Ich bin ein Berliner" speech given in Cold War Berlin. Through diligent research, especially on the Internet, it is possible to locate many historical speeches.

Music Music can include both songs and instrumental music. A colleague, in teaching a fourth-grade civil rights unit, highlights the traditional hymns and protest songs so intregal to the era. And when I taught a unit on the Native Americans of the Northwest coast, music was an important part of our study. Not only did we enjoy listening to tapes and watching videos of dances and singing, but my students enjoyed learning about the musical instruments.

Interviews Interviews and oral histories are powerful methodologies that children can easily manage themselves. My fourth-grade students have been doing immigrant oral histories for some years. One year, a colleague was being pressed by his students to allow them to watch a video of their choice in class. He sent them home to interview their parents about their favorite movies as children, and the one that the parents all liked the most was the one they ended up seeing, *The Nutty Professor* with Fred MacMurray. Paula Rogovin, a first-grade teacher in New York City, builds her entire curriculum around interviews.

Radio Shows Before television, radio provided all that we now expect from television. Radio archives offer everything from soap operas to news to drama, and some of these are available in text and audio formats. Children seem to quite love the idea of radio drama. A number of years ago a colleague taught an elective in which the children first listened to old radio dramas and then wrote and performed their own.

Objects

Household Appliances and Tools Every year I take my students to the Lower East Side Tenement Museum in Manhattan, a wonderful museum devoted to presenting the life of immigrants during the late nineteenth and early twentieth centuries. One of the museum activities is a guessing game, in which the instructor passes around objects and asks the students describe them and finally to try to guess what they were used for. By now I've observed this activity several times and know what the objects are, but I enjoy watching my students carefully studying them and then making cautious guesses. The objects are all household objects used by the tenement dwellers. The funniest for the children is, understandably, the chamber pot. Household objects like old iron or an electric 1955 toaster are easy to find and serve as excellent materials to help students investigate the past. They make tangible and real how different life in the past was in the most mundane ways. Having to use a chamber pot graphically illustrates for children the differences between life today and in the past.

Toys I played with dolls as a child, and I especially loved dollhouses. One of my favorite exhibits today is the dollhouse and toy exhibit at the Museum of the City of New York, which displays many dollhouses, each one reflecting the era in which it was made and the children who played with them. However, students don't need to go to a museum to find old toys. They've got plenty of their own. Their own baby toys can help children think about the past as effectively as older toys in museums. Certain toys seem eternal. One example is the yo-yo, which becomes enormously popular every few years. Stuffed animals have been a long-time hit, most recently manifested in the Beanie Baby craze. A visit to the Donnell branch of the New York Public Library provides visitors with the actual stuffed animals of Milne's Pooh books. Children can easily connect these well-worn toys to their own tattered animals and dolls.

Buildings Buildings represent an enormous category and a very important one. Buildings can include everything from a courthouse to a homestead. Looking at them is a powerful way to learn about the past. I spent time in many different schools and recall that in the older ones, it was often rumored that they had once had a swimming pool. I wonder if they all did actually once have swimming pools. I assumed not, but there was something so ghostly about the idea that there might have been one. At my current school, however, there was indeed a swimming pool in the basement at one time. It was removed long ago because of foundation problems, but one can easily see where it once was. The room-that-was-a-swimming-pool is entered through two doors and then small stairways down into the room itself.

Monuments On my last visit to Washington, D.C. I ran every morning on the Mall. I saw the monuments for the Vietnam and the Korean Wars, for Washington and Lincoln. Most interesting to me was the recently finished FDR Memorial. I recalled the controversies over its design, whether Roosevelt should be shown in a wheelchair (he isn't) and whether his beloved dog, Fala, should be presented larger than life (he is). Most communities have examples of monuments. In New York, we walk by many everyday without knowing who they honor. One around the corner from me is dedicated to one Franz Stigler (whoever he was). The most famous is the Statue of Liberty.

Clothing I have always been fascinated by the cyclical nature of fashion, the way clothing designers look to the past for what they hope will be the hottest new trends. Blue jeans are a perfect example. Developed in the nineteenth-century, these dungarees, blue jeans, or denims, as they are variously known, have become almost synonymous with America. Even as they go in and out of fashion in the United States, they continue popular throughout the rest of the world. A shrewd fashion historian would know when a pair was made. There were the rolled-up jeans favored by the 1940s and 50s bobbysoxers, the enormous hippy bellbottoms of the 1960s, the so-tight-you-had-to-lie-down-to-get-them on jeans of the 1970s, colored jeans of the 1980s, and the incredibly wide-legged baggy jeans of the 1990s. Antique clothing from a hundred years ago can be fascinating but children can also learn from garments stuffed in our bottom drawers and at the backs of closets.

Visual Material

Photographs Photographs are an easy entry into the past, especially those that are personal. Everyone seems to love photographs: on our walls at home, in albums, stuffed in boxes. Now photographs are no longer relegated to albums and occasional slides shows, but also appear on the Web as well. Photographs are also rich sources of information about past times. When I taught about the potlatch, an important ritual of many Northwest coast native people, photographs were some of our best sources of information about this ritual, which was suppressed for many years.

Films and Videos My parents most reluctantly allowed my grandmother to give us a television so they could view the Kennedy-Nixon debates. Otherwise, I'm not sure when we would have gotten a television. Even then, my sister's and my viewing was strictly limited to one hour a day. We found ways around that by going to visit friends, stepping out of the room during commercials, and telling my parents news "didn't count." Today, those old television shows are primary sources about the times in which they were made. Newsreels and news footage give students a novel perspective on war and peace. More and more oral histories are now being recorded on videotape than on audiotape.

Maps I have always loved looking at maps and making maps with my students. The Pilgrims relied on John Smith's map to find their way to the New World, and my students use this map in trying to figure out how the Pilgrims ended up on Cape Cod instead of near the Hudson, where they had intended to settle. It is interesting to look at world maps from different parts of the world. A map from the United States will have North and South American in the center, while a map from France will have Europe in the center. Maps can be more than geographical aids. The historians of the Luba people of Zaire, for example, use special memory maps, *lukasas*, to remind them of particular events in their past.

Fine Art Paintings, prints, and drawings offer yet another entry into the past. My students use seventeenth-century Dutch paintings to gain a sense of what life was like for the Pilgrims in Holland, where they lived before traveling to America. A painting by Bruegel, for example, provides some sense of this, especially the loose morals the Pilgrims deplored. The Pilgrims have been a popular subject of American painters for over a century, especially since Thanksgiving was declared a national holiday by Abraham Lincoln after the Civil War. However, the Pilgrims in these paintings are men and women of historical myth, not reality. My students enjoy studying these paintings, pointing out the inaccuracies, and considering why the painters felt obliged to pursue an idea rather than reality.

Places

Cemeteries Burial sites offer some of the most intriguing opportunities for children to explore the past. In New York City in 1991, an African burial ground was discovered in lower Manhattan during a routine excavation for a new building. Construction was halted while many tried to decide what to do. Archaeologists began a dig and discovered that this was the earliest African burial ground in the New World. Finally, the building plans were altered out of respect for the burial ground, and the building was finished in 1994. Now there is a memorial on the site, and an organization, the Office of Public Education and Interpretation for the African Burial Ground, has been created to provide educational tours and programs.

Cultural Landscapes Cultural landscapes are geographical places that resonate with history. Some, such as Gettysburg, Valley Forge, Colonial Williamsburg, Washington D.C., and Ellis Island, are well-known. However, many cultural landscapes are more personal. Some years ago I was taken on a walking tour of the neighborhood in Frankfurt, Germany, where my father was born and my grandparents and great-grandparents had lived. I knew that the family homes were no longer there. They had all been destroyed by bombs during the war. However, my guide, a German doing research on my family, had all their addresses, and the street names were unchanged. Up and down Leerbach, Kaiserhof, and Garnerweg we went seeking out house numbers that indicated the sites where the family homes had once been. I became a bit bored, but not my companion. Most determined, he found every location. He then pointed to a park and remarked, "That was where your great-grandfather's clinic was. I can now imagine exactly how he walked home for lunch every day!"

Parks From our great National Parks to the small park down the street, these outside spaces can tell us a lot about the past. The story of Central Park in New York is an extraordinary one, one of displacement of people as well as of a carefully designed landscape. Yet smaller parks have pasts as rich, if not as well known. Playgrounds are wonderful primary sources. They are so familiar to children that considering their changes over time can be an interesting way to study local history. Recently there have been several disputes in New York City over older adventure playgrounds, now considered too dangerous by today's parents. Together preservationists, architects, park officials, parents, and others have tried to reach a consensus on how best to preserve the architecture and yet make the playgrounds safe for today's children.

Questions & Answers

Q: Obviously you cannot always take your students to see original sources. Many are either far away or too fragile for the general public to view. So in many cases we are using reproductions. Are there issues associated with these reproductions that we should keep in mind as we teach?

A: Indeed, like most teachers, I use reproductions, of one sort of another, of many primary sources. When I taught the Maya I relied on slides, photographs, and videos to give my students some sense of their ancient cities in Mexico,

Guatemala, Honduras, and Belize. As part of another unit on the Anasazi, my students loved going to the gym to try out an *atalatl* (a spear-thrower) I had made at the Crow Canyon Archaeological Center near Mesa Verde in Colorado. The copy of the Constitution I use has been smoothed out with standardized spelling and contemporary punctuation. I search carefully for copies, reproductions, and facsimiles that I feel do justice to the originals. And as I do so, I keep the following constraints in mind:

1. Scale

   It is often difficult to communicate the scale of an object or place accurately . A friend told me about often seeing a colleague's paperweight version of the Rosetta Stone and being overwhelmed by the "dining room table" size, as he put it, of the original in the British Museum. On the other hand, I discovered after traveling to Central America that the videos and photos of ancient Mayan cities I had seem at home were very effective at communicating much of their grandeur and their context within the rainforest.

2. Quality of Reproduction

   While it is fun to have "old-looking" copies of the Declaration of Independence and the Constitution, it is worth considering how they looked when they were originally written. Is a fake "old" document going to help you achieve your objectives or simply provide a stereotypic view of the past?

3. Transcription

   Another primary source in my Pilgrim unit is William Bradford's memoir, *Of Plimoth Plantation*. The two edited versions I first came across were both redone with standard spelling and punctuation. While this made it easier to read, I was terribly curious about what the original looked like. I knew that the settlement was spelling three different ways, Plimoth, Plymouth, and Plymoth, and I wondered how other words were spelled. One day, browsing through our high school library, I came across an older edition of the book that retained the original spellings. It was fascinating to see the same word spelled three different ways on the same page (it made me wonder if I, always an abysmal speller, would have been better off in 1620!). I photocopied a few pages to show my students for fun, although I must admit I appreciate the more recent editions with their standardized spelling. It is important to be aware of how much has been "corrected" in a transcription.

Q: While the possibility of using primary sources in my teaching is exciting, the very idea of trying to find them seems overwhelming. Any suggestions on how to get started?

A: While I will offer suggestions for where to find primary sources throughout this book and in the accompanying CD, there is no way I can anticipate each individual teacher's needs. Anyone interested in using primary sources in their teaching must be prepared to do some investigating to ferret out materials. However, having done a great deal of it, I can assure you it is fun! The best place to start is the Internet. Not only are more and more primary sources being digitized and placed online, but companies and institutions with primary sources available for rent and/or purchase can also be easily found on the Internet. Certain institutions such as the Smithsonian, the Library of Congress, and the National Archives and Records Administration make available reproductions of many of their holdings. The Boston Children's Museum has a rental program offering eighty-nine Museum Teaching Kits on a range of topics. The kits are designed to encourage hands-on and active learning utilizing primary sources and other materials. One of their most popular kits is "Indians Who Met the Pilgrims," which provides students with various materials to learn about northeastern Wampanoags, both today and in the past. Other topics include Medieval People, Traditional China, Japan, and Ancient Egypt. More information is available at their Web site: <www.tcmboston.org/teachers/kits.htm>. Catalogues are available by calling: 1-800-370-5487.

Two commerical companies that offer facsimilies of primary source documents are Social Studies School Service and Jackdaw Publications. Social Studies School Service is a large catalogue company, which offers a wide selection of primary source materials for teachers. Information is available on their Web site: <www.socialstudies.com>. Jackdaw Publications specializes in kits of primary source documents on historical and literary topics. I've found the one on the Pilgrims tremendously useful. Although often geared toward secondary schools, these packets have materials that are excellent for upper elementary students as well. For more information visit their Web site: <www.jackdaw.com>.

3

From Personal to Local to the Most Remote Using Primary Sources in the Classroom

On our tour we walked through Chinatown, the Lower East Side, and Little Italy. We walked to old stores from the early 1900s and new stores too and filled our mouths with pistachios and Belgian fries. It was really fun, a new experience, and I learned a lot.

The thing I liked most about the walking tour is that it wasn't like all the other field trips where you have to follow all these rules. Like in a museum: don't touch anything, stay quiet. But here you were outside and you could do almost anything you wanted.

The walking tour was sooooo fun. My mom loved Gus's pickles. She picked me up for piano in the car and when we stepped out the car smelled like pickles. There were ten left although I got about fifteen and my mom called the 800 number for more.

September. I'm in my classroom unpacking boxes, trying to figure out which book orders have gone astray, deciding whether I want to put anything on the bulletin boards or wait for the children to fill them, and considering how to arrange the desks. The room feels unpleasantly empty. No children until next week and no sign of their presence yet through artwork, writing, toys, scribbles, and the like. To make myself feel better I organize my desk in the corner . My favorite books come first: those professional books I refer to frequently, great read-alouds, new children's books, a handful of nineteenth-century schoolbooks, a friend's self-published poetry books. Next my collection of things: mugs, figurines, key chains, drawings, photographs, even a cookie jar, all gifts from children. Much better; in this one corner at least, the room is beginning to come alive. More cheerful now, I tack up old class photographs for my nostalgic former students, certain to come and seek out signs of their presence in this classroom. In the meeting area I set up a book display and fill it with immigration books for our first social studies unit of the year. On a roll at last, I straighten up the classroom library, prepare a file cabinet for student portfolios, and label supply bins. With these teaching and learning artifacts in place, the room seems to wake up after its summer hiatus—and so do I.

As I put up the old class photographs, I idly look at myself over the years. I was thinner in 1994. What happened to that outfit I'm wearing in the 1995 photo? And how unchanged is my hair for the past three years—am I due for a makeover? Primary sources, I suddenly realize, these class pictures of the last few years are primary sources telling the viewer something about me and my class. They are personal primary sources, meaningful mostly to me and my students, but primary nonetheless. Cleaning out a cabinet I come across my New York City guidebooks, the ones we use for our walking tour of immigrant New York. I start paging through them, thinking about the way I might want to do the tour this year. Again I think, primary sources—the tour is full of buildings, signs, and other objects that tell us a great deal about our local and community history. At the computer I check my email and find a message from Gail Desler, a fifth-grade teacher in California with whom I'm collaborating on a project. She's writing to let me know that she has scheduled her class trip to Angel Island, the former immigration port of entry in San Francisco, for October 14th. Will this date work for our trip to Ellis Island? she wants to know. Gail and I met online and soon learned that our beliefs, approaches, and styles of teaching were very similar. After discovering that we both start the year with remarkably similar immigration units, we decided to have the two classes teach each other about these historic ports of entry on opposite coasts (primary sources yet again). And it finally becomes clear to me that I have a new focus: this school year of the millennium will be one of primary sources.

Centering the Curriculum on Primary Sources

For me every school year is new. Although the curriculum topics often stay the same, the projects and activities are always different, even if I've done them before. The main reason is that each new class of children brings unique personalities, learning styles, and knowledge to our classroom work. Their fresh views make it all new for me too. For example, for a number of years now I've done an immigrant oral history project. I've got the structural elements pretty well honed, but the unit is never the same. Each year, children bring their own ideas about how to approach the task as well as a new group of interviewees. Student teachers, volunteers, and parents all bring different perspectives to the project every year. New ideas about learning and new resources change my teaching.

My decision to focus on primary sources did not come out of the blue. My own alertness to original materials had been increasing over the years. And as I became more conscious of primary sources, I made my students more conscious of them. The summer of 1997 was a major turning point. As an American Memory Fellow at the Library of Congress, I considered how best to use primary sources in my teaching. During the following school year I referred to primary sources more often, not only when doing oral histories and reading firsthand accounts in our historical studies, but also in our literature studies. When we were studying *Alice's Adventures in Wonderland*, I pointed out that Lewis Carroll's photographs of the real Alice were primary sources. So, we realized, were E. B. White's early drafts of *Charlotte's Web*. The next year I went still deeper, using primary sources off the Web to connect my students' own oral history interviews to firsthand accounts by the Pilgrims. All this talking about, thinking about, and reading about primary sources produced an epiphany of sorts for me: this year I decided I would introduce primary sources from the beginning and have students consider and use them not only in history but throughout the curriculum.

Personal Primary Sources

"How was the trip?"

"Wonderful! Do you want to see some of the photographs?"

"Of course!"

"Well . . . if you are sure. Okay, here we are at our hotel. It was really, really nice! And this one, oh that is one of the kids in front of Buckingham Palace. And this one, isn't it great? Everyone said Venice would be dirty, but it wasn't. It was beautiful. See, can't you tell from this great photograph?"

Show and Tell. We do it all the time, not just in school. Whether we are modeling a new coat, showing snapshots of a recent vacation, or telling a long story about our weekend, we are bringing the personal artifacts of our lives to others. Show and Tell has long held a sacred place in the school day. It provides a chance for each child to take center stage, to bring something from home, and to tell everyone else about it. Although we may not all call it Show and Tell any more, many teachers still find ways for students to bring these personal primary sources into their classrooms and into the curriculum. Sometimes it can be a story. I'll never forget a child coming in one morning and telling us of a horrible fire in his apartment building. Fortunately, he and his family were fine, but his first-person account brought home to all of us, in a way no television news story ever could, the terror of such an event. Sometimes it can be a beloved book. When we visit the kindergarten, I ask my fourth graders to bring along their favorite books from when they were in kindergarten. Even as I write, a much played with toy castle sits in my classroom along with a tiny Cinderella, two stepsisters, and a fairy godmother (for some reason the prince has been lost), brought in by a student to enrich our study of fairy tales. Another student has brought in a Cinderella book she wrote in second grade to add to our collection of books. Personal artifacts of every sort can enrich classrooms in myriad ways. Those of us who believe in child-centered classrooms are constantly looking for ways to bring the home into the school, and personal primary sources are a wonderful way to do so.

Useful Personal Primary Sources

Photographs I've used personal photographs in many ways. For a student struggling to find a compelling topic to write about, a family photo album can provide the necessary inspiration. Children enjoy creating personal timelines with photographs of themselves at different ages. A "now" and "then" bulletin board can be fun to create with baby pictures and photographs of students today. I regularly take photographs of special events and field trips and then display the prints on our classroom door, as a reminder of the recent past. Often my students use photographs in remarkably creative ways. For example, Rebecca recently created a diorama showing her vision of *Charlotte's Web* as a movie. The background consisted of a hill with the well-known Hollywood sign on top, and in front, the familiar barn with all the animals. As for Fern, Rebecca had decided that she should play her and had put a small photograph of her own face on Fern's as she sat on the side watching the animals.

Collections Kieran Egan, an educational philosopher especially interested in the role of the imagination in learning, believes that eight- to fifteen-year-olds have a particular compulsion to learn as much as possible about a particular topic and recommends planning instruction to take advantage of this enthusiasm. "We see this kind of of detailed exploration in the obsessive hobbies or collections that reach a peak during this period" (1990, p. 85). His comment reminded me of my own collections as a child: dolls, miniatures, books, baseball cards, and rocks. I also have long observed this collection fervor among my students. A few years ago, many a backpack was full of keychains and children loved discussing these collections with me. More recently, Beanie Babies were the desired collectible, and I've learned more than I ever needed to know about which ones are worth the most, which have been retired, and so on. This age group's obsession with acquiring Pokémon cards received national attention when parents complained that it was akin to compulsive gambling. Inviting children to bring in their own collections or to start a class collection is another way to introduce personal primary sources into the classroom.

Polls and Interviews I often poll my students on a particular topic and record their answers on charts that I display about the room. As the school year goes on, the classroom fills up with these charts full of quotes from children. As we begin our fairy tale unit, for example, I write down every child's first stab at defining a fairy tale. The chart stays up even as the children learn more and the definitions change. At the end of the unit we return to the chart, and each child decides if his or her definition still stands. Sometimes the polls are more ephemeral. Before beginning a new chapter in the book I'm reading aloud, I'll often ask each child to predict what will happen. In the immigration unit, an elaborate oral history interview forms the core, but smaller interviews are useful too. I interview each child about his or her learning several times a year. The children also enjoy doing interviews. Some years ago, as part of a larger unit in which the children were learning about the school, each interviewed a staff member and we compiled the results into a "Who's Who" of the school.

Family Lore By family lore I mean personal stories, heirlooms, and rituals. It is very important to be careful when inviting children to bring in anything from home. Many families enjoy and relish the idea of their lives becoming part of the classroom curriculum, but others do not. Projects like creating a family tree can be enormously difficult and uncomfortable for some when all the data are not available or the project brings up hurtful memories. However, there are many other ways to bring family lore to school. In *Keepsakes: Using Family Stories in Elementary Classrooms*, Linda Winston describes a number of successful ways teachers have done so, including family sayings, recipes, mementos, and interviews.

The Name Project

I wanted to start the year with a new writing project. For some time I had begun the year by pairing the children off and having them interview one another and then use the information to write short author blurbs similar to those on book flaps, but it had started to seem old to me. With my interest in focusing on primary sources from the start, I came up with an new idea: a project built around how the children got their names. After all, their names were personal primary sources, weren't they? Investigating the history of one's name seemed a safe project for the start of school. All the children, no matter what their skill levels or family circumstances, were sure to have something to communicate about their names.

I had done a name research project some years earlier and unearthed it as I thought about this new one. I also emailed Gail Desler, the fifth-grade teacher in California with whom I was doing the immigration ports collaboration, telling her of my idea to begin the year with a name project. She responded immediately: "It almost gives me chills to read how you start the year—I think we must have worked together in a past life." Gail, it turned out, had already developed and taught a names research project. She sent me her assignment and I took several ideas from it as I developed my own. I had been interested in having the children interview family members about their names (primary source) and use books to find out about the derivation of their names (secondary source). Gail gave me two interesting ideas: using baby name books for the secondary research and using the chapter, "My Name," from Sandra Cisenero's *The House on Mango Street*.

That first week of school was one of talk and, frankly, a lot of that talk was mine. I had so much to say. My students were new to the building, so there was a lot to be explained: fire drills, lunch procedures, even where the bathrooms were. The children and I were equally relieved when such orientation was behind us and we could finally get to what we were really there for—the learning. Finally, the day came when I introduced the Name Project.

I began by writing *primary source* on the board and asked the children to tell me what it meant. "First," declared Nick. "Something to do with elections?" puzzled Nathaniel. "Original," posited Elizabeth. Delighted, I next wrote *secondary source* and again asked definitions. This time there was some confusion. It was difficult, the children realized. While they could give me examples of secondary sources, defining what it was stymied them. With my prodding we eventually began to define both terms. We decided that a primary source was as close to the real thing as possible, while a secondary source only told about the real thing.

After handing out the materials for the Name Project (see Figure 3–1, p. 41) I read the introduction aloud, reviewed the different parts of the project, and then told the children that I had already done the first part as a model for them: I had interviewed my father about my name. I then read them the following notes from this interview:

> Look for names with sounds that would go well with Edinger. If you were a boy you would have been David, so before your birth we called you Davida. We wanted to give you two names: a common name and an uncommon name. For the common name we picked your middle name, Ruth. I felt my own name was uncommon (Lujo for Ludwig Joachim, which he changed to Lewis when arriving in the U.S.) so wanted to spare you that. We knew no one in this country with the name Monica. People always wanted to know if it was spelled with a *c* or a *k*. It was more common in Germany and England. Of course, the name has now caught up with you (Monica Lewinsky).

That day for homework the children interviewed their parents about their names. Many came in the next day surprised about what they had learned. I asked each to share one note from their interview with the class. We then proceeded to the next step: researching with secondary sources. For that, I showed the children how to look up Monica in several baby name books. One did not have my name, while two did. From these two I took the following notes:

THE NAME PROJECT

We care about our names. Given to us by our parents, they soon become our own. Sometimes they change, become shortened, or altered into nicknames. Sometimes we like them and sometimes we don't. However we feel about them, they are still ours alone.

For this very first writing project you are going to explore your name. You may already know a lot about it, or you may be surprised by what you discover. Either way, it is bound to be fun and a great way for you to introduce yourself.

Researching Your Name
Primary Source Information
A primary source is getting as close to the original as possible. In the case of you name your best primary source informants are your parents. After all they gave you your name. Find out as much as possible about why they named you as they did. Are you named after a relative? If so, why? Were you named for some other special reason? Try to find out as much as possible and write down your source (your parent or anyone else you ask about your name) at the end.

Secondary Source Information
A secondary source is farther away from the original. In the case of your name it might be some background about your name. Use the baby books in the classroom to see what you can find out about your name. If the baby books do not have your name we will see what other secondary sources might be available to help you. Write what you find out in the space below. Don't forget to write down the source (book) from which you get the information.

Thinking About and Describing Your Very Own Name
Listen to a reading of "My Name" from Sandra Cisenero's novel, *The House on Mango Street* and discuss the different ways she describes her name. Then write down your own creative descriptions of your name.

Writing About Your Name
Now use all the information you collected about your name to write an interesting paragraph about your name. Be sure to provide an interesting lead to get your readers interested and a way to end the paragraph as well. Use the space below to write your first draft. Once finished, read it over and revise it. Then have a conference with a teacher, do a final edit (your teachers will show you how), and a final draft on another piece of paper.

_____

_____

_____

_____

Figure 3–1. The Name Project Handout

- Latin: advisor or counselor
- Greek: merit
- Irish: noble
- Was popular in 1940s and 1950s esp. among Catholic families (maybe because of St. Monica from 4th century).

The children enthusiastically began researching their own names. In addition to the baby name books, we discovered a terrific site on the Internet <babyzone.com> full of factual information about names. Using this site and our baby name books every child was able to find out something about his or her name.

For the next lesson I read "My Name" aloud from *The House on Mango Street*, by Sandra Ciseneros. Together the children and I discussed this short piece. They noted the following:

- Esperanza Cordero doesn't like her name.
- It sounds like tin in English, she says, and like silver in Spanish.
- Doesn't want to turn into her great-grandmother, for whom she was named, one of those women who "sit with sadness on an elbow."
- She is envious of her sister Magdalena, who can also be called Nenny.
- Feels her name evokes the number nine and a "muddy color."
- Makes her think of the Mexican records her father plays while shaving, "songs like sobbing."
- Wishes she could rename herself Zeze the X.

We then spent five minutes writing down our feelings about our own names. Here are mine:

Disliked it as a kid. Too weird. Badly wanted a nickname. Decided Micky would be good. No one else did, though; best I got was "Mon," which was bad too. On the first day of fourth grade I told my teacher that I used my middle name, Ruth, but then was too shy to ever answer to it.

The only Monica I ever knew as a child was a Monika in Germany, the child of family friends who played far too rough for my taste. It seems, however, that suddenly in the last few years there are Monicas everywhere. It feels very strange to me after growing up never running across any in real life or even in books. Just yesterday I overheard someone in the street talking of a Monica. It is still hard for me to feel that it is someone else they are speaking about.

Monica feels like the color red and makes me think of the old Beetles' song, "Michelle," probably because that name seemed close to Monica when I was young.

Now we were ready to pull this material together into a short essay. Again, I first modeled the process by writing a draft about my own name. I showed the children exactly how I would take some of the data, but not all of it, and even add in new details to make an intriguing story. My first draft:

> After feeling like the only Monica in the world for most of my life, I suddenly am one of many—famous Monicas and infamous Monicas. It is a terribly strange sensation to hear someone else being called Monica. How ironic! I used to hate that no one else had or even knew the name and now I hate how known it has become.
>
> In fourth grade I told my teacher to call me by middle name, Ruth, then was too shy to answer. You see, my parents gave me two names: Monica Ruth—a common one and an uncommon one. Guess which was which?
>
> Today I prefer Monica. Ruth seems pretty dated—but not when I was nine. Anything seemed better than Monica then. I tried for nicknames—Mickey seemed good, but the best I ever got was Mon.
>
> Do you spell it with a *c* or a *k*? people wanted to know. Well, I sure didn't want to be anything like the one Monika I knew, a rough playmate in Germany.
>
> Today I'm a teacher and find it only right that Monica in Latin means advisor and comes from a fourth-century saint. Maybe I'm no Saint Monica, but at least I'm certainly no Monica Lewinsky either!

The children then worked for several periods on their own first drafts. When they looked ready for the next step, I did a minilesson on revising with Julia Stokien, the learning specialist who works with me several periods a week. I demonstrated reading over my first draft and making revisions. Then we modeled a conference, and Julia made several suggestions about how I could make the piece clearer. The children then worked in a workshop setting until they reached the final stage: editing. Again I did a minilesson demonstrating how I would do this with my writing. Finally we all produced publishable final copies, which I put on the Web for Gail Desler's fifth-grade students to see. They had done a similar project, and she posted their name pieces. Both classes were able to learn a bit more about each other as individuals. I also took photographs (which I did not put on the Web, nor did I put the children's last names on the Web for safety reasons) and created a bulletin board display outside the classroom door just in time for our fall Parent Open House. Of course parents and children very much enjoyed this! Even put away into portfolios, these name stories still intrigue them and are bound to become important primary sources, and maybe even family heirlooms, some day.

Elizabeth

I have always liked my name but I would tell some people my name was Halley. That is my middle name. My mom and dad were either Emily or Elizabeth. I am happy that they picked Elizabeth. It's not that I don't like Emily but it's hard for me to think that's what my name could have been.

I always hear people on the street yell my name and I turn around and think that they're talking to me. I have learned over the years it is normally someone else.

When I was little I would think that just cause I had the same name as Queen Elizabeth I could just go and meet her. One day I wrote to her and never got a letter back. I found out I wasn't going to see her.

There are a lot of variations to name Elizabeth. One is Elizabeth to Isabelle which both come from Elizabell that means oath of the gods. I love my name and wouldn't want to be named anything else.

Zach

My mom thinks that the name Zach is charming and strong. She met a great Zachary in college who was smart and went to Harvard. That was the first Zachary my mom ever met. My dad got Zachary from his Grandfather Zussman. He was an immigrant who started a fruit and vegetable company. At one point he had the biggest fruit and vegetable company in the United States. That is how my mom and dad picked the name Zachary for me.

Growing up I like and dislike the name Zachary. I like the name because it has great nicknames. Also, to me, Zachary sounds like great things, like all the things that I like. I dislike the name Zachary because there are so many ways to spell it. All the time people ask me how to spell it. Also now there are so many Zachs. When I was young and growing up I was the only Zachary around.

Today I am nine and most people like my name. There are still a lot of Zacharys. That doesn't stop me from liking my name. To conclude, I just want to say again, "I like my name. My name is my own."

Local Primary Sources

I live and teach in New York City, where I'm often overwhelmed by the huge number of opportunities for learning. We can go to Ellis Island, the Lower East Side Tenement Museum, and visit the historic and still thriving immigrant neighborhoods nearby during our immigration unit. Smaller communities can also offer an equally rich palette of primary sources for teachers and students. Recently, I spent some time in Wellfleet, Massachusetts, on Cape Cod. I visited the Wellfleet Historical Society and chatted with the president, Betty Cole. The Society, I discovered, displayed only some of its many primary sources, from old photographs to instruments to toys. Mrs. Cole told me that the Society worked with the town's elementary school, providing artifacts for children doing local research. Every year, the Society lead a historic walking tour, and in 1995 the Wellfleet Historic Society and the Wellfleet Elementary School joined together to create a guided walking tour of Wellfleet's main street. They produced a charming small book, *Looking Back at Wellfleet*, to go with the tour. Mrs. Cole reported that the tour has been very successful and that the Society has worked closely with the school to support children and teachers in their studies of local history. Similar opportunities are available within driving and walking distances of most of our schools.

Useful Local Primary Sources

Landscapes Landscapes consist of both natural and man-made features. Whether you live in an urban or a rural community, landscapes offer potent possibilities for primary source investigations. At the end of our study of the Pilgrims, we take the whole Dalton School fourth-grade class to Plymouth, Massachusetts. We spend much of our time at Plimoth Plantation, a living history museum recreating the 1627 original settlement. After visiting this recreation it is fascinating to go to the site of the original settlement, described in the Pilgrim's accounts. One can easily see why they selected this particular location. Particularly impressive is walking up Burial Hill and seeing where their first buildings were. The features of the natural landscape that caused the *Mayflower* passengers to settle here are still visible; the nearness to the ocean, a stream of freshwater nearby, a hill from which it would be easy to keep watch.

Man-made landscapes are also intriguing primary sources. In New York City we can simply walk down any street and discover many sources of information about the city. One that is often overlooked is street furniture: benches, street lights, fire hydrants, telephone booths, bus stops, and the like. How these change over time can tell children much about the past. For example, many fire hydrants are no longer used. My students are fascinated to observe that in Chinatown the telephone booths have a unique Chinese style. Later in the chapter I will describe a walking tour of lower Manhattan, during which my students document the man-made environment with photographs.

Maps I love maps and try to find every opportunity to use them in my teaching. In 1999, while I was thinking about our annual downtown walking tour, I decided we would look at maps of New York from different time periods. Excited, I called the research department at the Lower East Side Tenement Museum, but my hopes were dashed when my informant told me there were few maps that showed the changes over time. After all, the street names haven't changed; it is the buildings that have changed, and they aren't usually indicated on maps. I sought out the old guide books he recommended and discovered that he was right: the maps looked remarkably similar to contemporary ones. Knowing that reading a map of any kind would be challenging, I have given up on my idea of having students look at old and new maps for the time being. They still intrigue me and I'm sure that one of these days I'll figure out a way to use them. Certainly, if I lived in a community where maps did show change over time, I would undoubtedly use them with my students.

Newspapers New York City is full of newspapers, from the *New York Times* to free neighborhood weeklies. I find it fascinating to look at old newspapers, but even current ones are full of interviews, photographs, and other information.

A Walking Tour of Lower Manhattan

Walking tours are one of the most successful ways to explore local primary sources. They can be as simple as taking a walk around the block studying the landmarks close at hand or going a bit farther afield, in my class's case, to lower Manhattan.

Several years ago, I began teaching my current social studies curriculum, which focuses on immigration. I had heard of the Lower East Side Tenement Museum and quickly made a plan to visit, as did my four grade-level colleagues. One of them, Sarah Gribetz, immediately took the experience a step further by planning a walking tour of the neighborhood around the museum as well. I loved the idea and have used it for a number of years now, revising and improving it each time. The structure I have devised would be equally suitable for a class walking tour of a different neighborhood on a different topic.

We go in November after weeks of immersion in the study of immigration. By this point my students have been to Ellis Island, begun their own oral history immigration interviews, and read and heard many books about historical and contemporary immigration. They have a strong factual foundation of information. For the tour I tell them we will be walking through a historically significant immigrant community of New York City—the Lower East Side, Chinatown, and Little Italy—and to be on the lookout for signs of old and new immigration. They easily see vestiges of the past in signs of old shops and new ones as well. Old signs are often in Polish, while new ones are in Spanish, for example.

Teacher Preparation Every year I spend a great deal of time researching and preparing materials for the trip. For the first one I looked at a number of current New York City guide books to see which aspects of the three historic neighborhoods they featured. I also looked for a map that would cover the three areas and still be easy for my students to read. When I found one, I added numbers to identify special places of interest and provided a key. Every year I revise the list (see Figure 3–2, pp. 47) to add new places and drop old ones. This year, my new colleague, Gini Noble, found an even better map and several new and intriguing places to visit.

Next, I make up groups of three or four children. They will be walking for two hours accompanied by one or more adult chaperones (parents love this trip, and I encourage as many as are able to join us). I find that groups no larger than four work best, but I certainly realize that most public school classes are much larger and that it may not always be possible to have as many chaperones. Of course,

---

WALKING TOUR

1   **The Tenement Museum**
97 Orchard (between Broome and Delancey)

1a   **First Roumanian American Congregation (Synagogue)**
Rivington between Orchard and Ludlow

2   **Katz's Delicatessen**
205 E. Houston (Corner of Ludlow)

2   **Bereket Grill House (Turkish food)**
187 E. Houston (at Forsyth)

3   **Yonah Schimmel (knishes)**
137 E. Houston (at Forsyth)

4   **Old St. Patrick's Cathedral**
264 Mulberry (between E. Houston and Prince)

5   **Italian Food Center**
186 Grand (at Mulberry)

6   **Ferrara (Italian pastries)**
195 Grand (between Mulberry and Mott)

7   **Fong Hing Bakery, Inc. (Chinese pastries)**
Hester Street (between Bowery and Christie)

8   **Rong Kang Chinese Herbs**
Hester between Allen and Eldridge

9   **The Lobster Farm**
87 Hester Street (corner of Allen and Hester)

10   **The Sweet Life (Fruits and Nuts)**
63 Hester Street (Ludlow and Hester Streets)

11   **Gertel's Bakery**
53 Hester Street (between Essex and Ludlow)

12   **Guss Pickle Products**
35 Essex (between Grand and Hester)

Figure 3–2. Walking Tour

New York City is a busy, crowded place. For parents and children to feel secure, these small groups are necessary. A different type of community might require a different type of configuration: In a place like Wellfleet I might find high school students to act as chaperones in addition to adults.

Student Preparation The day before the trip I give each child a copy of the map and a list of places to visit. First I orient them. Where are we going? I ask. Where is lower Manhattan in relation to our school? I am always pleased when they are able to tell me that it is south and way at the end of the island of Manhattan. Dalton is located at 89th Street between Park and Lexington Avenues in a neighborhood known as the Upper East Side. Lower Manhattan is quite unfamiliar to most of my students. In the neighborhood around the school, the streets are often numbered and laid out in grids, so it is remarkably easy to find one's way around. However, Little Italy, the Lower East Side, and Chinatown are in the oldest part of the city where the streets have names rather than numbers, and they are not always laid out in an easy-to-navigate grid.

To be sure each child can read the map, I ask them to highlight the streets that border the walking tour area as well as the streets they would be using during the tour. In order to be sure they highlight the correct streets I have one already completed as a model. I then have them locate and clearly mark on the map the Lower East Side Tenement Museum, where the tour starts and finishes.

One of the highlights of the tour every year is the opportunity to try different kinds of food. The children each bring ten dollars, which is sufficient for lunch, dessert, and other snacks along the way. Over the years I have figured out which places are best for a quick child-friendly lunch. Best of all are places with quick service. The favorite is invariably Katz's Delicatessen—a quintessential old Jewish place full of grumbly employees, wonderful signs, and terrific pastrami sandwiches, matzo ball soup, and other standards of Jewish cuisine. Fortunately, they also do a terrific hot dog, which is by far the most common choice of the children. On the same block as Katz's in 1999 (who knows what will be there in 2000 because things change quickly in Manhattan) are a Japanese restaurant, bagel shop, pizzeria (New York is well known for selling pizza by the slice), Indian restaurant, Belgium fries take-out place, and a Turkish fast food spot. This diversity shows the changing immigrant patterns of the neighborhood. Katz's and the bagel shop are vestiges of the earlier community of Eastern European Jews, while the other places show newer immigrant groups who have come to the neighborhood more recently. I give the children an overview of the different lunch possibilities and ask them to decide beforehand as a group where they want to go to. I also recommend other highlights, such as a synagogue, a church in Little Italy, a Buddhist temple in Chinatown, and a variety of interesting shops.

In groups the children negotiate where to have lunch (sometimes they go to two places to accommodate different tastes) and which places they don't want to miss. I remind them that I have mentioned only some of the interesting places to visit and that they must be on the look out on their own for more. I also remind them to look up: often the most interesting signs are above street level.

Parent Preparation Each group has an adult chaperone, usually a parent but sometimes a school staff member. A week beforehand I send home a letter carefully describing the tour so they know what to expect on that day. I warn the parents and children to dress for two hours of walking, and for possible bad weather. On the day of the trip, before we leave the school, I review all aspects of the day with parents and children together. Each group receives a "one-time use" camera for documenting any indications of immigration they see. Each group also receives a folder with maps and basic information about the trip (including emergency phone numbers). The children are encouraged to collect as many primary sources as possible along the way; I recommend they ask for take-out menus, business cards, flyers, printed napkins, and whatever else businesses along the way are willing to give them.

The Walking Tour Itself: Collecting Primary Sources The trip has been an enormous success each year. The children are well prepared and enjoy leading their parents on the tour they've planned. The parents are elated and I frequently receive notes afterward attesting to their great pleasure with the trip. Often they do the tour again on a weekend with other family members, the children acting again as proud tour leaders. This past year a parent told me her daughter wrote a long letter to her grandfather the evening after the trip and they would be sure to replicate the tour for him the next time he came to visit.

Every year I take one group myself and have great fun encouraging the children to try unfamiliar foods and to go into Chinese herb stores, or pointing out laundry on a tenement fire escape that looks like a scene from one hundred years ago. For many of us this is a new neighborhood, and we explore it like tourists. The children love to collect artifacts: business cards, menus, catalogs, and flyers. Most end their trip at Gus's Pickles and the bus ride back is invariably full of the smell of dill and vinegar.

Upon our return to school, I always ask the children for brief initial reactions to what they've seen. Again and again they have told me that what they liked most of all was the sense of freedom. Never before had they been on a field trip where they were so much in control. On previous trips to museums and other places, everything they did was carefully planned. This had been amazing to them; a trip where they were in charge! One child, unfamiliar with the lower part of Manhattan, commented that he felt like he was in another country, not his own

Figure 3–3. Hester Street in 1904

city. Certainly, Canal Street in Chinatown was a revelation for many students. Everyone seemed to look Chinese or be speaking Chinese, and all the signs were in Chinese. Another child spoke of how much fun he had following the map. And still another spoke of how fascinating it was to explore so many different ethnic establishments, that the range of New York's immigrant history came home to him in a way that no book reading or video viewing could possible do.

Synthesis and Analysis: Creating Secondary Sources The following week I give each group a large piece of poster board along with the folders of materials they had collected and the photographs they took and I challenge them to document their tour in a poster. We discuss the fact that they will be creating secondary sources: interpretations of the trip and the materials. They have a wonderful time organizing their project; thinking about how best to communicate all that they saw in the streets around them: a sign advertising a school that teaches English to new immigrants, a Chinese noodle factory, live eels at a Chinese market, an Asian restaurant in an old Polish bank . . . every year new images.

We end our unit by having each group present their poster. The class loves this part because each group's unique experience has much to offer the rest. Then I put the posters up on the wall for the rest of the year, documents of immigration in lower New York and of my students' learning.

Photographs Then and Now

While searching for old New York maps I discovered *New York Then and Now: 83 Manhattan Sites Photographed in the Past and Present* (Watson and Gillon 1976) I was especially intrigued to discover two photographs of Hester Street viewed from Essex Street, one taken in 1904 and the other in 1975 (see Figure 3–3 and 3–4), and I realized that we passed this corner on the walking tour. Studying the two photographs, I could see that many of the buildings were still the same even if the shops had changed. I made copies of the two photographs and asked students to take a new photograph at the same site during the walking tour (see Figure 3–5, p. 53). The following week they carefully studied the three photographs.

Figure 3–4. Hester Street in 1975

Group Members: *Josh, Matthews, and Nathaniel*

Comparing a Lower East Side Street Scene over Time

(Hester Street West from Essex Street)

1. Compare the photographs from 1904 and 1975. What do you see in both photographs?

1904	1975
1. smaller buildings	Bigger buildings
2. Less stores	More stores
3. More people/less wagons	Less people/more cars
4. Lighter (color) bricks	Darker bricks
5. Less buildings boarded up	More buildings boarded up for storage
6. More peddlers	no peddlers
7. more people on street	less people on street

2. Compare the photographs from 1904 and 1999. What do you see in both photographs?

1904	1999
1. Cobblestone road	Paved road
2. Small buildings	Skyscrapers
3. More people on street	No people on street
4. Less transportation	More transportation
5. Bigger windows	smaller windows
6. More street furniture	Less street furniture

3. Compare the photographs from 1975 and 1999. What do you see in both photographs?

1975	1999
1. American stores	Imported stores
2. Less cultures	More cultures
3. Less street furniture	More street furniture
4. Old clothes	Modern clothes
5. More people	Less people
6. Older cars	Newer cars

What can you conclude from these discoveries? (Write your ideas on the back.)

Figure 3–6. Comparison Chart

52

Figure 3–5. Hester Street in 1999

When Josh, Matthew, and Nathaniel analyzed (see Figure 3–6) their three photos, they drew the following conclusions:

1. Windows were bigger in 1904 and 1875 than in 1999 because it was fashionable.
2. Less people walked on the street as time went by. More cars on street.
3. More stores as time went by. More people, more stores.
4. Roads got smoother as time went by. Need smoother roads for new cars.
5. More cars/transportation as time went by. More people need more transportation.
6. Less street furniture as time went by. Need more room for cars and transportation.
7. Less peddlers as time went by. Illegal to sell things in street without a license.

Remote Primary Sources

As a child I moved around a lot because my father was a roving academic. I was born in the South but spent my elementary and early high school years in the Midwest and Europe. Because I had traveled so much, I prided myself on being open toward other cultures. However, when it came to Africa, my knowledge was limited and stereotypic: Albert Schweitzer (the Mother Teresa-icon of my childhood) helped sick people there, people lived in grass huts, elephants and giraffes lived there. I have absolutely no memory of ever studying Africa in school. If I did, not a trace remains.

In 1974, I applied to the Peace Corps. I requested an assignment in Africa or Asia. As I waited to hear from the Peace Corps I developed a list of further requirements: I wanted to learn a new language, there should be no snakes, definitely a dry climate, and plenty of game parks, please.

In the midst of the Watergate crisis I received my invitation to teach in Sierra Leone, a country I had never heard of. A former British colony on Africa's west coast, Sierra Leone's official language was English, the country was riddled with snakes, it was mostly tropical rain forest, and there were absolutely no zebras. The invitation put my sentimental notions to rest: "Peace Corps service is not a junior year abroad nor a romantic adventure . . . The Peace Corps in Sierra Leone does not exist for the benefit of volunteers, but rather for the benefit of Sierra Leoneans . . . So come to do a job, not to find yourself." On August 9, 1974, I flew off to Freetown, Sierra Leone leaving behind a resigning President Nixon and my preconceived notions of Africa.

Those two years in Sierra Leone affected my subsequent life in profound ways. Africa is no longer a faraway, exotic place that moves in and out of my consciousness as it moves in and out of the news. I'm very cautious about judging circumstances, cultures, and situations that are substantially different from my own. Stereotyping, cultural relativism, explicit and implicit bias, and the many issues of living in a multicultural world are always with me as I live my life and as an educator. I try to find ways to bring my Sierra Leone experience into my teaching so that Africa is less exotic and unreal to my students. I look for teachable opportunities: the Civil War, immigration, world geography, or current events; anything that seems appropriate. And when I do talk about Sierra Leone, I do so almost exclusively with clothing, art, photographs, artifacts, and my memories of living there. Seeing the traditional cloth of one of my well-worn dresses, moving fingers across shiny cowry shells, paging through school books, and studying photographs of my home, my friends, and favorite places give my students a larger view of the world.

Useful Remote Primary Sources

The Internet The Internet provides a window into the world, to those places that once seemed remote and inaccessible. Virtual field trips are a good way to help children learn more about other places. These online adventures offer a range of primary sources: videos of rain forests, photographs of cities, sounds of dance rituals and other traditions. Done carefully and sensitively, such online field trips can deepen students' understandings of other people and places. Done superficially and carelessly, they only reinforce preexisting stereotypes. Email relationships offer the same potential and peril. Children can build genuine relationships and gain new knowledge about peers in other countries. They can also, if insufficient context is provided, simply reinforce preexisting stereotypes with such relationships. Some years ago, when I was teaching a unit on the Maya, I discovered a weaving cooperative in Guatemala through the Peace Corps Partnership program. My class raised money for the cooperative and exchanged letters with the members. In addition, the Peace Corps volunteer sent me a videotape she had made of the cooperative. The relationship personalized my students' studies of the Maya, past and present. I have no doubt that similar kinds of relationships could easily be established via the Internet. The important element is making the connections deep and meaningful.

People Resources I strongly encourage teachers to investigate their local community to locate people who are from, or have lived for substantial periods of time in, the places students are studying. Letting people know is often all it takes. Returned Peace Corps volunteers are a particularly useful resource.

I would advise teachers to be aggressive and tenacious. Several years ago, when I was teaching a unit about the Native people of the American Northwest Coast, a colleague told me of a relative at the University of Chicago Lab School who had discovered a button blanket maker in a book, tracked her down in British Columbia, and received a grant enabling them to bring her all the way to Chicago. Inspired, my colleague and I decided to do the same. We applied and received a PTA grant and hosted Marion Hunt Doig for a week in New York City. She brought button blankets, artifacts, instruments, and her stories. Our classes that year experienced an understanding and closeness to the people of the Northwest Coast unattainable to those classes who did not have the chance to know Marion firsthand.

Forced Immigration Project

When I first conceived of the fall immigration unit the most important goal was to provide a multicultural perspective. In the school where I teach, the majority of families are descended from Eastern Europeans who came through Ellis Island.

However, this was not the family history of all the families in our school's community. And, it was only one perspective on the vast history of immigration to the United States. I was adamant about creating a curriculum that provided personal insight into the immigrant experience and a view that went beyond Ellis Island. I was interested in the issue of how to ferret out historical truth through oral histories. This is how the oral history project became central to the unit.

For many years the unit was different every year, although the central activities remained the same. Each year's class had their own family histories. Sometimes the vast majority were of Eastern European descent, but often there were also children with Asian, Latino, Western European, Australian, and African backgrounds. A recent class included several African American students, and I considered anew how best to bring forced immigration to the fore. Fortunately, one opportunity came through the cross-continental project with Gail Desler's fifth grade class in California. Her class visited Angel Island, an immigration port primarily used to detain Chinese immigrants, on the same day my class visited Ellis Island. Each class then sent the other questions about the port they had visited. One, from Gail's class, asked: Had Africans come through Ellis Island? My students and I struggled to find an answer. It seemed that most of the immigrants were European. However, one day, we came across a photograph of some African immigrants at Ellis Island. "Maybe they were first in Europe," commented one of my students, noticing the very western style of clothing.

Our conversations about immigration more and more involved Africa and slavery. The contrast between those who came by choice and those who came by force was striking to my students. Building on their interest, I decided to read *In the Time of the Drums*, a picture book retelling of a Gullah ghost story that, as the author's note relates, was passed down orally over generations. Although the author describes the Gullah as related to Nigerians, others have suggested a connection to Sierra Leone. Joe Opala, an anthropologist who served in the Peace Corps in Sierra Leone with me, has studied the similarities between the Gullah language and culture and those of Sierra Leone, and concluded that there is ample evidence to suggest that some of the Gullah were originally from Sierra Leone. After reading the story, I mentioned some of the memories of Sierra Leone the story evoked for me. Then I gave the children small cards and asked them to write down one thought the story evoked for them related to our ongoing conversation about primary sources, about our new unit on Cinderella, or about immigration. The responses were fascinating. The children made remarkable connections, noting that the story was not quite a primary source because it had been altered through its multiple retellings and by the author's own creative telling of the story. There was some consideration of whether it was a fairy tale, like Cinderella, or something else. Many were disturbed by the images of the slaves in chains and how different that was from the relatively benign images of crowded Ellis Island ferries.

As we discussed the book and mulled over the Middle Passage compared to the worst steerage class, the class was stopped short by one African American student who insisted that the slaves' journey was not as horrible as that of those who came to Ellis Island. How could he say that? other children wondered. It was dirty, he insisted, they were so crowded, so miserable. Many children tried to change his mind. Another African American boy recollected his visit to a museum in Maryland that was full of exhibits about the Middle Passage. When nothing would change his mind, I realized that many of my students had very little sense of forced immigration. Their visit to Ellis Island was a powerful, direct exposure that emphasized the difficulties of these journeys. They had been further moved by learning about Angel Island from Gail Desler's class, where Asian Americans had been detained during the years of the Chinese Exclusion Act. Particularly disturbing to many of my students was a film about Proposition 187. This 1996 California law (fortunately never enacted) denied health care, schooling, and other basic needs to undocumented immigrants. My students were terribly disturbed by the injustices of Angel Island and Proposition 187. However, our conversation after *In the Time of the Drums* made me very aware of how little they knew about the unique horrors of forced immigration for the enslaved Africans who had no choice in the matter. I needed to give more attention to this issue.

Olaudah Equiano I decided to read Ann Cameron's (1995) adaptation of Olaudah Equiano's autobiography, *The Kidnapped Prince*. Equiano was kidnapped in 1755 at the age of 11 from his village in Benin. He begins by lyrically describing his homeland. Much of his description sounded so similar to Sierra Leone that before I knew it I was showing my photographs of Sierra Leone to the class. He wrote of palm wine and I described it to my class, the sap of the palm tree gathered as one does maple syrup, something my students were familiar with. He wrote of a "berry to dye the cotton a beautiful shade of blue. Everybody, men and women and children, dressed in this blue cloth. Later in my life I went to many places, but I never saw that special shade of blue" (p. 5). I then pointed out the blue cloths from Sierra Leone I had tacked up on the classroom bulletin boards. This indigo may well be the blue he meant, I told the class, very common throughout West Africa even today. He wrote of traditional slaves, and my students learned that slavery was not solely a European activity but traditional in Africa as well. He described his home, and again I showed photographs similar to his written description. Olaudah described how he was kidnapped, sold repeatedly, and brought far from his homeland to the coast. He wrote of the scarred people he encountered, and I spoke of the ritual facial scarring that was quite common when I lived in Sierra Leone. The children and I also talked about plastic surgery, so common in our culture, to recognize that scarring wasn't as strange as it first appeared. He wrote that for money, "the people used little white sea shells, the size of a fingernail" (p. 21), most likely cowry shells, I thought, and showed the class a handful from Sierra Leone. As Olaudah is brought closer to the coast, he encounters iron for the first time, an indication of European contact. I showed the children iron pieces that had been used in Sierra Leone during this time as money in addition to cowry shells. My artifacts and memories of Sierra Leone enhanced and enriched Equiano's story.

The description of Equiano's ocean journey put an end to my student's idea that those who came through Ellis Island had it worse. I had watched this student as I read, worried that he might be too shocked, and curious about how he would respond. He was riveted. It was clear that this was all new to him. After a few days, another child asked him if he had changed his mind. Indeed he had. He did not doubt now that this had been far, far worse, that in fact, the two experiences could not even be compared.

When I reached the point in the narrative that described a slave auction, I asked the children to record their responses thus far in their weekly journal letter to me. Here is what several children wrote:

> I'd say I definitely disagree with Tom. When you write to him have him make a chart [like this] of the odds and evens of Ellis Island and being a slave.

Slave	Ellis Island
tight boat	feel well
sold	not the best beds, but at least there were beds
couldn't move	
bad food	movable
treated like you were an object	taken care of

> One of the things I hate about history is that people can't have freedom. When you read a book like this many other people besides me probably think, "It's not fair. People deserve to have freedom." People don't need to be treated like kings, but they should have their share of happiness. If people are so happy, they should help other people be happy, but not by using them as a machine.

> The Kidnapped Prince is probably one of the hardest books to be written. When he [Olaudah] wrote it, it must have been hard to remember all this. The biggest thing that this story makes me think about is try to put yourself in his position, think about it for a while. See what happens to you. Even though this happened to him, now I want to go to Africa. It seems like the place of glory.

The Kidnapped Prince is fantastic; it is very hard to believe that stuff really happened. I was overjoyed to see all the stuff that you brought from Sierra Leone and I thought that it was *beautiful*!

Benin While I was reading *The Kidnapped Prince* I met Wendy Smith, Educational Director of the International Rescue Committee. A long war had been going on in Sierra Leone, and I had contacted her to ask if there was some way I could help Sierra Leonean refugees. As we conversed I discovered that she had been a Peace Corps Volunteer in Benin, Equiano's homeland. I told her about our study and asked if she might be willing to visit the class to speak about Benin. Her firsthand account of Equiano's country today would be of great interest to my students. She agreed with enthusiasm. A former teacher, she missed contact with children.

Wendy visited my class with an assortment of primary sources on Benin, which provided an even more interesting view of Equiano's homeland. She showed them a videotape that had been made in the town where she lived, gave out maps of Benin and pointed out where she had lived (and where Olaudah may have been from), taught the children a few phrases in Bariba, played music from Benin, and had children try on clothing from Benin. Both Wendy and the children had a wonderful time. She ended by showing them a quilt honoring the different royal kings of Benin, each symbolized by an animal. She asked the children do special homework for her, to write what animal they would be and why. Many children did this and I sent their writings on to Wendy, along with my thanks for her vivid look at Benin, the land Equiano had come from.

Sierra Leone In May 1999, months after we had completed our immigration studies, Sierra Leone reappeared in the news, at war again. I had been following the situation closely, but had not felt it was appropriate to discuss with my fourth graders. The images of atrocities and child soldiers were horrible. However, during a morning meeting Josh mentioned that he had seen that Foday Sankoh, the rebel leader, had been captured. He remembered our conversations from the previous fall about Sierra Leone and wanted to know more. As we began talking the children asked what they could do to help. Before I knew it we had a whole project underway. My students' grave concern and thoughtfulness for the people of Sierra Leone moved me. After some consideration, we decided to have a combination exhibition/bake sale. The exhibition would help others in our school community learn more about this small West African country and the bake sale would raise funds to help the people of Sierra Leone. The children went to work learning all they could about Sierra Leone for the exhibition. Photographs, books, and artifacts from my life in Freetown were resources as were Web sites. The final bake sale and exhibit were very successful, both in raising money and awareness for Sierra Leone.

Questions & Answers

Q: You seem to enjoy using your own personal primary sources with your students. However, not all of us have the family history or travel experiences you have had. Can you give some tips to help us know what from our own and our student's lives we might use as primary sources in our classrooms?

A: I like to keep stuff and recommend that other teachers do so as well. Of course, it isn't always easy to save stuff. In my case, I'm very limited in storage space as I live in a very small New York City apartment. Nonetheless, I've managed to find space for old high school art work, notebooks from college, and even a file of re-sumés dating back to the mid-1970s (goodness knows where that will come in handy, but you never know!). In a closet next to boring, but neccessary, financial data is a large file with all the paperwork of my Peace Corps term from the very first invitation to join to a document entitling me to health care if any of my trop-ical ailments recurred when I came back to the States. Elsewhere are clothing, cooking utensils, toys, art, photographs and books from my time in Sierra Leone. While I hope I'll never be audited and thus never need the financial data, I often pull out my Peace Corps material when speaking about Africa or when reminisc-ing with other former volunteers.

Some of my personal primary sources are not nearly as interesting as the ones I've saved from my time in Sierra Leone. At the start of every school year I talk about how I learned to read. That I didn't do so until second grade, when I was in Germany, my mother patiently tried to help me learn to read in English while in school I was also learning to read in German. The transforming book was a British paperback my parents had picked up in England for me, Monica Hugh's *My Naughty Little Sister* (having an irritating little sister was, no doubt, the appeal). I still have that very book, which I show to my students along with my German reading book and various notebooks in which I was learning to write both in script and with a fountain pen. These primary sources intrigue my students, as does my old fourth-grade class picture. Only rarely is someone able to figure out which child is me!

But I'm not the only one contributing personal primary sources to my class-room. My students love to bring objects, texts, and visual material in from home. I've asked children to bring in the first book they ever loved, primary sources from their earlier school years, and baby photos. Personal primary sources are some of the easiest to find and use in the classroom.

Q: You live in New York City where there are incredible local history resources. How do you suggest those of us who live in smaller communities find local resources?

A: Studying your local community is a wonderful unit at different grade levels. Primary sources to support such a unit exist in abundance. I'd suggest investigating municipal archives, local newspaper morgues, and historical societies. Then there are the best resources of all: people. I highly recommend doing oral histories. Not only do these provide students with value information, but their informants may lend them copies of passports and alien registration cards, old photographs, and other materials to supplement their oral histories. The children are always respectful and careful with these precious materials.

Q: Okay, you've traveled a lot and are very alert to what's available all over the world. What about those of us who don't do so much traveling; how can we find remote primary source resources?

A: I think one of the reasons I did not even think about using primary sources when I first started teaching twenty-five years ago was that it was before the era of photocopying. I relied on books for information and ditto machines to make copies of my assignments. I think my interest in using primary sources in the classroom dovetailed with easier access to photocopying. I generally made copies of primary sources that I came across in books and articles. Once I had access to a VCR at school, I began taping public television programs for use in my classroom too. If I felt they were worth using in future years, I would buy them through companies like Social Studies School Service. I now have, for example, a good collection of videos about the Maya, Tlingit, and Kwakuitl. I collected artifacts through my travels, but I also knew of museums that had artifact lending kits one could order through the mail. Often colleagues, parents, and friends had artifacts they would bring to school. For example, some good friends of my parents collected Hopi kachina dolls and once brought some of their collection to my classroom.

With the Internet, access to remote primary sources has skyrocketed. It seems that every institution of significance has a Web site. American Memory is one of the largest digitized archives at present, but other institutions, such as the Peace Corps, are creating online sites rich in resources, making it possible to easily gain access to a remarkable range of primary sources about places distant in time and space.

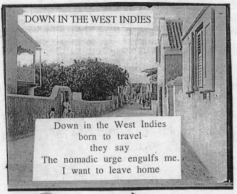

DOWN IN THE WEST INDIES

Down in the West Indies
born to travel
they say
The nomadic urge engulfs me.
I want to leave home

I hear and read a lot of America

People say it is a "bed of roses."

I want to go!   I want to go!

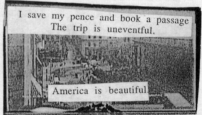

I save my pence and book a passage
The trip is uneventful.

America is beautiful.

I
go
into
the
tall

office

buildings

on

lower

Fifth

Avenue.

I try them all.

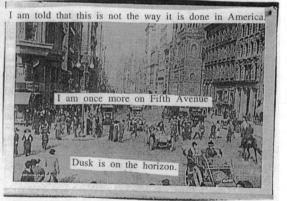

I am told that this is not the way it is done in America.

I am once more on Fifth Avenue

Dusk is on the horizon.

I am black,
foreign looking
I am smiled out.

4

Pig Iron and Ranches
Beyond Ellis Island with American Memory

> I learned that people went to places like ranches and went on boats with pig iron and came to different parts of America not just New York.
>
> I learned that people immigrated not only to Ellis Island, but to other places.
>
> I learned that so many people came over as farmers and were so different from what we learned before and what I thought immigrants were when they came over.
>
> I learned that immigrants did not always come to NY but to the Mississippi and a lot of different places and immigrants did not always come for a new life.

A famous *New Yorker* magazine cover by the artist Saul Steinberg shows a New Yorker's view of the world. In it, Manhattan is huge, and the further away from New York, the smaller and more insignificant the place. As someone who is from one of those insignificant places I try to make my fourth graders aware that New York is not the center of the world, while still encouraging them to learn as much as possible about this large city that is their home. Thus, their experiences during a lengthy study of immigration include visits to immigrant neighborhoods as well as Ellis Island, oral histories of recent immigrants as well as readings of historical fiction, and discussions of current events that affect immigrants throughout the country. My hope is that students develop a sense of the range of people who came to America, the many reasons for their immigration, and the complexities of assimilation. However, most of the newcomers the children encounter, whether a Russian whose family came in 1884 or a Jamaican who came in 1994, end up as New Yorkers, and thus the urban images of sweatshop workers, pushcart peddlers, and tenements have dominated their view of U.S. immigration. It took the farmers, stonecutters, and cowboys of the American Memory Web site to push them beyond the frame of Saul Steinberg's New York-centric world to an expanded understanding of American immigration.

American Memory

American Memory is a Web site maintained by the Library of Congress National Digital Library Program. It includes an every increasing number of digitized primary sources from the Library's vast holdings and from other major research collections. These unique on-line collections include American history documents, films, manuscripts, photographs, sound recordings, and maps. The variety of the available collections is enormous and grows constantly. Highlights include materials from the Constitutional Convention, Walt Whitman's notebooks, panoramic maps, Civil War photographs, California folk music, oral histories, and early motion pictures.

In addition to placing these materials on-line and offering excellent support services, the Library has also reached out to K–12 educators in many ways. One was the American Memory Fellows Program, which has allowed teams of middle and high school educators to develop lessons using the American Memory online collections. Fellows do much of their work on-line, meeting at the Library itself for one week during the summer. Curriculum units developed by American Memory Fellows are available on-line through the Learning Page, an area of American Memory devoted to supporting learning at all levels.

In 1997, the first year of the program, I teamed up with Cory Brandt, then library director of the Dalton School, and joined twenty-four other teams from all of over the country as American Memory Fellows to develop curriculum using the American Memory Collections. Cory and I created History Firsthand, a fourth-grade library/social studies curriculum that was used with all Dalton fourth-grade classes during the 1997–98 school year.

History Firsthand

History Firsthand came out of conversations that Cory, a trained archivist, and I had been having about the fourth-grade library program. The children had always had weekly library classes in which they learned to use the card catalogue, what a bibliography was, and other traditional library skills in addition to being read to and having time to browse. But Cory, the middle school librarians, and I had become aware that the program needed to be revised to accommodate the newer information literacy skills the children needed as they began using the Internet more and more. We all agreed on the importance of keeping the read alouds and the browsing time, but an overhaul of the other research-related activities was long overdue. The opportunity to revitalize the program using the American Memory Web Site seemed perfect, and the result was History Firsthand.

It was designed, as Cory and I wrote in our Introduction, "to provide elementary children with experiences that will enable them to better understand the complexities of primary source collections and how to do on-line research. Moving from personal artifacts to the vast American Memory collection, students learn about how collections are organized, how to interpret artifacts and documents, how to use primary sources to tell a real story and how to effectively search on-line collections." Cory used his background as an archivist to create lessons that would help the children better understand such collections, while I used my classroom experience to help connect these activities to the children's personal experience and to the classroom curriculum. In addition, History Firsthand was grounded in U.S. immigration, a major theme of our fourth-grade social studies curriculum.

Cory and I explored many American Memory collections looking for materials on immigration that would be appropriate and accessible for fourth graders. Since the collections are all primary sources, many of them can be quite daunting, even for an adult. After a we'd spent time browsing many different collections, we decided to use three for our unit:

Inventing Entertainment: The Early Motion Pictures and Sound Recordings of the Edison Companies
http://memory.loc.gov/ammem/edhtml/edhome.html
Cory and I originally used a collection (Early Motion Pictures, 1879–1917) that was subsequently reconfigured into several separate collections, of which this was one. The Edison collection includes more than 200 motion pictures as well as 80 sound recordings.

American Life Histories: Manuscripts from the Federal Writers' Project, 1936–1940
http://memory.loc.gov/ammem/wpaintro/wpahome.html
A wonderful collection of 2,900 oral histories from people all over the country, including eyewitnesses to the Chicago fire, pioneers, factory workers, and immigrants.

Touring Turn-of-the Century America: Photographs from the Detroit Publishing Company, 1880–1920
http://memory.loc.gov/ammem/detroit/dethome.html
A collection of more than 25,000 photographs that are often sold to other companies to make postcards and calendars. This vast collection includes images of buildings, natural landmarks, vehicles, cityscapes, and even photographs of paintings.

History Firsthand ended up having three parts:

Unit 1—Personal: What is a Collection?
The section consists of activities built around the children's personal interests to help them learn more about the attributes of artifacts and primary sources. One librarian, in teaching the unit, had the children use their shoes as a way to determine attributes. They grouped them by size, color, and brand as a means of thinking about how collections can be organized in different ways.

Unit 2—Local: How are Collections Organized?
This section moves the children beyond their immediate world to that of their school. These lessons focus on the organization of archival collections. The Dalton librarians gave the children a number of materials from the school's archives such as photographs, yearbook pages, letters, and even financial statements. Children were then asked to appraise these documents, to determine if they were worth keeping in the archives or discarding.

Unit 3—National: Searching an On-Line Collection
Unit 3 moves the children to the national level to a focus on American Memory. Having now gained an understanding of archival work, they are to focus their attention and their knowledge of how to search for and use materials in selected collections to help develop a story about immigration. The site and collection were was introduced by the librarians using the Early Motion Picture collection. The children used the keyword "immigration" to search the American Life Histories Collection. They used the keyword "immigration" again, as well as other words, to find photographs of the immigrant experience in the Detroit Publishing Company collection. Their final step was to combine the American Memory material with their knowledge of immigration from their classroom work to create a poster.

Teaching History Firsthand

During the 1997–98 school year, the middle school librarians taught History Firsthand as part of their weekly library classes. Cory oversaw the program and I consulted as needed. The first unit proceeded successfully, but problems came up in the other two units. The appraisal activities in Unit 2 were very difficult for the children. They struggled to make sense of the Dalton School archival materials they had been given and were unable to determine what should be kept and what discarded. Unit 3 got off to an unfortunate start when we were unable to download and use the films as planned and had to jump to the next lesson. The children thus delved into searching the Life History Collection without sufficient modeling beforehand. The manuscripts turned out to be extremely challenging for the children to read. Most successful were their searches of the Detroit Publishing Company collection. But even then, they generally focused on Ellis Island photos and made little effort to find other immigrant-related images. Their final posters were disappointingly simplistic, showing none of the rich learning about the immigration experience that I knew had occurred in their classrooms.

Assessing History Firsthand

At the end of the school year, Cory left Dalton. Eager to see what could be done to salvage the program, I met with the middle school librarians and fourth-grade teachers for their honest assessment of History Firsthand. All agreed that, while it was worth retaining, it needed a major overhaul. In particular, they felt that the unit needed to connect more closely with the children's classroom experiences; they also thought that the activities needed more scaffolding so that the children would be more invested in their work—and ultimately more successful in the learning outcomes Cory and I had originally envisioned. Finally, we decided that I would revise History Firsthand this time as a classroom-based unit and use it with my class during the 1998-99 school year. The result was a totally new unit: Found History.

Found History

Excited about having a second chance with American Memory, this time with my own class, I decided to continue with the immigration theme of History Firsthand, because the site is particularly rich in these materials. I also knew that the children needed to spend a great deal of time studying immigration first. With a firm foundation in the topic, they would be able to deal with the challenging American Memory materials far more successfully. Finally, after a great deal of thought, I decided that the new unit would consist of a project, a way for students to demonstrate their understanding of immigration, which they would already have been studying for several months.

An important aspect of all my teaching units is the final product. Carol Ann Tomlinson (1999) defines such a product as "a vehicle through which a student shows (and extends) what he or she has come to understand and can do as a result of a considerable segment of learning" (p.43). While I believe firmly in children "constructing" their own learning, I also think they should have a tangible result to show what they have learned. Through the years, my students have produced books, charts, posters, magazines, Web sites and performances. For History Firsthand, the children had made posters using U.S. immigration photographs from the

Detroit Publishing Collection, one of the American Memory collections. I had found these posters disappointing because, despite their attractiveness, they focused on the particular immigration experience of Ellis Island. One of the reasons I had thought the American Memory collections would work so well with our immigration curriculum was that the children studied all sorts of immigration stories, not just the Ellis Island story and American Memory was full of these many different stories.

Despite my dissatisfaction with the posters, I thought something combining text and images would be a good final product for the new unit, yet how to get the children to move beyond Ellis Island would be a challenge. They would need something to inspire them—what, I did not know.

Fortunately, through my work as a facilitator during the 1998 American Memory Institute, I met Alison Westfall and Laura Mitchell, whose idea of using the WPA Life Histories Collection to create "found poetry" (poems created from snippets of text from previously published material) gave me the inspirational hook I needed. While poetry isn't my strong suit (I admit there isn't nearly enough of it in my classroom) I loved the idea of found poetry and knew my students would too. I decided that the children would search the Life Histories for immigration transcripts and then use them to create found poems that evoked the immigration experience they had already been learning about.

I next considered how to bring a visual component to the project. I knew I wanted the children to search the Collections for photographs to illustrate their poems, but I also knew that I wanted them to do something more with the photographs than just stick them on posterboard with their poems. The posters from the previous year's History Firsthand unit had seemed visually dull. This time I wanted something more creative, something that would meld art and history as the found poetry did. The solution came to me as I was browsing through the Detroit Publishing Collection. I came across several colorized photographs and it occurred to me that one of the reasons the posters the year before had been so bland was that all the photographs had been black-and-white. The children could find black-and-white photos and then color them using those in the Collection as models. In fact, there was nothing to stop them from cutting up their copies of the photos (downloaded from the Web), using sections and parts of different images to illustrate their poems. In other words, they would make collages consisting of their found poems and photographs: Found History.

Now I turned to the issue of structuring instruction. The American Memory Collections are demanding. Even adults can feel overwhelmed attempting to search them, so how much more a nine-year-old. I knew I would need to structure each encounter with American Memory carefully so that the children would feel successful, not frustrated. I decided to be sure that within each lesson I would:

- Introduce the collection and activity by connecting them to the children's prior knowledge.
- Model each activity before the children did it.
- Be sure the children had a good understanding of how to proceed with a particular activity before they began.
- List all procedures on charts and handouts for the children to have nearby as they worked.
- Continually review the procedures, especially from one day to the next.
- Try to anticipate all technology problems and be prepared for the worst.

I carefully worked out a sequence of lessons and then made all the necessary arrangements to gain access to the computer lab. The Dalton Middle School Computer Specialist, Kristin Sternberg, was very enthusiastic about the project and made a point of being available for most of the lessons. This was enormously helpful, since the children often had to use computers in different rooms, and having two adults at hand made it easier. Kris was also able to troubleshoot as needed. I probably could have coped on my own, since I was determined to do the project, but her presence was extremely reassuring.

Teaching Found History

Prior Knowledge of Immigration I began the unit by telling the children that I wanted to see if they could recall all the immigration activities they had done since the start of the year. I wrote them down on a class chart and then followed up by asking them to tell me some of what they had learned. Of course, not every general idea we covered ended up on the chart, but enough came out to convince me that they had a solid understanding of the basic ideas and issues underlying much of U.S. immigration historically and today.

What We Have Done and Learned About Immigration

What We Have Done
- Read immigration books (e.g., Karen Hesse's *Letters from Rifka*, Bette Bao Lord's *In the Year of the Boar and Jackie Robinson*, and Kathryn Lasky's *The Night Journey*).
- Interviewed immigrants and created picture books based on the interviews (oral history project).
- Watched videos.
- Completed a mini-project: Immigration ABC Posters.
- Made a trip to Ellis Island to view exhibits and visit oral history library.
- Took a Walking Tour of Lower East Side documented by photographs.

- Visited the Lower Eastside Tenement Museum.
- Studied the citizenship process.

What We Have Learned
- That America means something important/special for immigrants before they come.
- That it was very hard for many to come.
- That Ellis Island was very hard to go through.
- That it was hard to make a living, find a home, etc.
- That people came for many reasons: job, school, persecution, war, famine, for a better life, religious freedom, political freedom, to join family, because of natural disasters, for economic reasons.
- That people made changes after coming in their names, language, and customs.
- That people used different forms of transportation.
- That the poor, who came on boats had terrible experiences.
- That families were separated (deportations, not all came, some died).
- That tenements were small.
- That people came from many different countries.
- That the reasons for coming weren't always bad.
- That immigrants brought their cultures with them to America.

Primary Sources Introduction When I introduced the term *primary sources* to the children, they had not heard of the phrase before, but easily understood the idea. Throughout their immigrant oral history project, they had been very conscious of the need to be absolutely true to the words of their subjects. Thus, it was easy for them to understand the idea of firsthand information and how to distinguish it from secondary information.

The Library of Congress Now came the Library of Congress, a rather big idea, but one the children were able to grasp. The knew what a library was, after all, and the idea of a very large one that held everything published in the United States impressed them no end. We discussed some of the many functions of the Library before moving on to American Memory.

American Memory Using a large monitor with an Internet connection, I finally introduced American Memory. The children were all quite familiar with the Internet, so the idea that the Library of Congress would place some of its materials on-line was obvious to them and less amazing than for adults who grew up before the Internet existed. I gave the children a tour of the site, especially to confer a sense of the range of materials the collections contained. The Baseball Card Collection and those on the presidents made the greatest impression. I was pleased the next day when several children easily and correctly described both the Library of Congress and American Memory.

Inventing Entertainment: The Early Motion Pictures and Sound Recordings of the Edison Companies For the next lesson I focused on a specific collection. I had selected a motion picture collection because I wanted the children to experience a range of media in using American Memory. Also, earlier in the immigration unit I always showed a number of Charlie Chaplin films, including *The Immigrant*, a short in which Chaplin parodies the well-known images of the poor immigrant in steerage, going through Ellis Island, and making his way in the world. The children were thus very familiar with the old black-and-white films of this era, and likely to be intrigued by those in this particular collection. I had been disappointed the year before that we had been unable to use the motion pictures and was very excited about being able to do so this time around. Fortunately, with Kris's help, we had none of the technical problems of the previous year.

I first gave children an overview of the collection. They were amazed to think that these films, created so long ago, existed. I then told them we would search for films that could give us more information about immigration. Using the keyword "immigration," I found three films. Two were of Ellis Island and the third of an "arrest in Chinatown." (The Library is always adding to their collections. When we did this lesson in 2000, the sound recording "Don't Bite the Hand That Feeds You," also came up in our search. After completing our analysis of the motion pictures, we listened to this song and discussed its virulent antiimmigration lyrics.)

Now we came to the evaluation aspect of on-line searching. One of the most insidious aspects of searching on the Web is that it is so hard to determine what is worthwhile and what is not. Snazzy graphics and sound can easily convince a viewer of accuracy. I wanted the children to realize that just because these films were old and firsthand information, that did not mean they were equally worthwhile.

We viewed each film. The children easily decided that the two Ellis Island films provided worthwhile information about immigration. They were full of fascinating material, some of which caused my students to alter their previous ideas about immigration. Many of the disembarking passengers in one film actually looked quite middle class. The women wore hats rather than the kerchiefs so prevalent in Chaplin's film, and the children had previously seen many of the photographs of turn-of-the-century Lower East Side. There were more children and less baggage than they expected. However, turning to the Chinatown film we came across something quite different. It was a very short film of someone (presumably Chinese, but it isn't really clear) being arrested in San Francisco's Chinatown. The only information we had about the film was the bibliographic data from the time, and "arrest in Chinatown" was all it offered. We watched it a number of times but still had a hard time even figuring out who was being arrested, much less learning anything about immigration. Ultimately, the children decided that of the three films, only the Ellis Island films were helpful in learning about immigration.

American Life Histories: Manuscripts from the Federal Writers' Project, 1936–1940 The next series of lessons focused on the American Life History Collection, manuscripts rich in the voices of their times. The variety is stunning. Some writers carefully maintained the voice of their subjects, while others produced highly subjective third-person reconstructions. While the writers were provided with guidelines, they clearly followed them loosely and used their own writerly techniques as well. For my students, who had done their own oral histories, much of the language of these texts was familiar. They knew all about doing interviews and how to transcribe them. They had each, after all, quite recently spent hours listening to their own tapes, carefully transcribing every word. They could also understand the range of these manuscripts because they had chosen to represent their oral histories in picture books. Still, these Life Histories were quite different, most notably in that they weren't done for children but to record the stories of everyday people. As a result, some were quite graphic—violent, racist, sexist, full of drinking and gambling. Many of these people had led hard lives and their attitudes, could be quite shocking for a contemporary ten-year-old. From the start of our work with the Life Histories, I warned children to expect different sorts of dialect, words, ideas and language than they were used to. Fortunately, the manuscripts the children ended up using were relatively mild, although they were nonetheless taken aback and amused when someone used a "dammit" or spoke of drinking.

Modeling the Process I began by telling the children that we would be creating *found poetry*. A found poem, I explained, was similar to a collage. A visual artist makes a collage by collecting interesting bits from newspaper, magazines, and other sources, and then assembling them into an aesthetically appealing image. In the case of a found poem, the poet first has to search for a text that is full of interesting words. The poem is then constructed out of these unique words taken from the text. In other words, a found poem is a sort of word collage. To further aid their understanding, I read several examples of found poems from Annie Dillard's collection, *Mornings Like This*.

For our found poems we would be using manuscripts from the Life History Collection. To begin, I showed them how to search the Life History for a manuscript that was about immigration but was also appealing to them. We would be searching among many manuscripts for just the right one that struck us as lyrical and that had poetic potential. Our next step, after finding such a manuscript, would be to turn it into a found poem.

Using the large monitor, which all the children could see, I went to the American Memory search page and typed in the keyword "immigration," which quickly produced thirty-four manuscript titles. The titles were a jumbled group. Some were names, while others were more obscure ("These Two Things" or "Mysterious Chinese Tunnels").

You had to go into several manuscripts files I explained, and search through them to see where the word *immigration* appeared. When I put the keyword "immigration" in, I explained, all that meant was that the word was somewhere in the manuscript. It was necessary to skim through the manuscript searching for the keyword in boldface. I did this with several manuscripts, some that were clearly not about immigrants and some that were. "Mysterious Chinese Tunnels" turned out to be about tunnels under the city of Seattle that may have been used to smuggle in immigrants. Eventually I selected "Noboddy Boddas You," which I had preselected to use to create our group found poem.

The complete manuscript for "Noboddy Boddas You" follows. We found it on the Library of Congress, American Memory Web site. It is shorter than many others that come up in our search but typical in what it leaves out. Some manuscripts provide lots of detail, while others are full of omissions. For example, there is no way to know the name of the person only that he is the restaurant's manager being interviewed. The words are there but his name is not. Nonetheless, it was a perfect example for my students because, like their oral histories, it is a direct transcript in the first person. It also takes place on Orchard Street on the Lower East Side of Manhattan, a place familiar to the children. While ambling about that old neighborhood they had searched for signs of old and new immigration and this manuscript easily evoked feelings of old immigration. Beliska's Restaurant, where the interview took place, is long gone, but Katz's Delicatessen on Delancey, where the children had lunch, is still thriving. The language of the anonymous speaker of "Noboddy Boddas You" is not unlike the cadences still heard at Katz's and other establishments of the Lower East Side.

Subject: "NOBODDY BODDAS YOU" (Beliksa's Restaurant)

Come in gentlemens, sit down I got here a nice table. You vant better to sit over here—[Louis?], clean off!—is de same price. A pot of tea, right away. Here is evvyboddy velcome. Vot kind of people is here? You see. Dere is pushcart peddlers, a few contractors, bricklayers, maybe carpenters., painters a few. Heff and heff: heff is voiking, heff on relief—homerelief you call dis. Her noboddy boddas you: for 5 cents a day you sit, for a pot 10, 15 cents for two people. You play cards; do vot you like, so long you don't disturb. No, dey don't play for money; just for de treat. Is hungarians, Russians, de same faces, always the same, business is steady, ven somebody dies is vun less. Since de immigration is closed, you know, it grows gradjally less people; it is shrinking, yes, buisness is shrinking liddle by liddle.

Voices: Stop hocking a chynig (Quit clapping on my kettle). . . De vater gets cold already . . .

—Excuse me please gentlemens, later I come back, not I am busy.

* * * *

(Note: I was directed to the tea-room by one [ccp?] and a couple of pushcart-peddlers on Orchard Street who told me it was a real old-time joint and insisted that the "tie" was drunk there from pitchers. The tearoom, known as the Beliska Restaurant, is located on the first floor of a building undergoing demolition at the corner of Delancey and Orchard. Seated at ancient tables along the walls and upon a platform in the [?] are gesticulating merchants and peddlers who drink tea from glasses and bite inot [cubes?] of sugar while they play a "[shtiekel pinechle?]" or discuss affairs in Europe. It is all an interesting "joint" and the following rough transcipt of the manager's friendly conversation is merely to set the locale for stories which I hope to gather there in the future.)

First I modeled how I would read through the manuscript. I thought aloud as I went, showing exactly how I would try to make sense of the text. For example, I guessed that "heff is voiking" meant "half is working." I considered what it might mean to be able to sit in a restaurant all day when out of work with a pot of tea for very little money. Once satisfied that the children had a good sense of the text, I opened a word processing file and cut and pasted the text into it. Then, with advice from Kris and the children, I moved words and text around, cut extraneous material, and worked and reworked the poem until we were all satisfied with it.

NOBODDY BODDAS YOU
Come in, gentlemens,
sit down I got here a nice table.
A pot of tea, right away.
Here is evvyboddy velcome.

pushcart peddlers,
bricklayers,
contractors,
carpenters,
painters
a few.

74

for 5 cents a day you sit,
for a pot 10,
15 cents for two.

hungarians,
Russians,
de same faces,
always the same,
ven somebody dies is vun less.

Here noboddy boddas you.

Searching the Life Histories At the next session I reviewed the previous day's process with the children. They had been delighted with "Noboddy Boddas You." I put it on our classroom door so many teachers and students had read it and enjoyed it already. They were eager and ready to begin working to create their own found poem. We began by reviewing the steps taken to create the poem. We read the poem out loud, then we returned to the original manuscript and looked at exactly which words we had taken and discussed why. Moving back even further, we reviewed the steps taken to find the manuscript in the first place. These would be the same steps the children would now use as they sought out manuscripts to use themselves for their own found poems.

After this review the children helped generate the following chart listing the strategies they had observed me using while I read through the manuscript and those we all had used to create the "Noboddy Boddas You" found poem.

Life Histories
Objective/Goal: Pick a life history and make a found poem that has something to do with the immigrant experience.

Strategies to help understanding:
• Check dictionary, atlas, etc.
• Use context before/after unfamiliar words
• Skip material that is too difficult—you don't have to read every word.
• Work as a group.
• Ask a teacher for help.
• Pint out and read a manuscript away from the computer and use a highlighter to mark parts that you might want to use in your poem.

Strategies to help create a found poem:
• Keep the beat.
• Consider shape, order, and line length.
• Consider your beginning/end.

The children's contributions to the chart assured me that they were ready to work on their own poems. I divided them into groups of three or four and gave them the handout shown in Figure 4–1. They then went to the computer lab to begin their own search.

The groups worked hard. They were a bit shocked at first to discover that most of the manuscripts were long and they had to work through them to find whether they were immigrant stories or only about immigration. "Noboddy Boddas You," one child noted at the end, "seemed more like a poem right from the start." Once a group had selected a manuscript, they returned to the classroom and read through it to consider what it meant. They then used highlighters to select possible words and phrases for their poem.

AMERICAN MEMORY
SEARCHING FOR LIFE HISTORIES

Goal: To find ONE Life History from an immigrant. You will be using this oral history to create a found poem, as we did with "Noboddy Boddas You."

1. Go to the American Life Histories Page.
    http://memory.loc.gov/ammem/wpaintro/wpahome.html

2. Select *Search by Keywords*

3. Search full text using the keyword: *immigration*

4. You will get 34 documents (on two pages).

5. Browse as many documents as you can. First look for where the keyboard "immigration" comes up. Is the document about an immigrant or not? If not, don't spend time on it. Move to another one. Remember, they may be difficult to read—full of dialect, perhaps racist stuff, even bad language. Don't be surprised and don't let it interfere with your task—to find the best document possible for a found poem.

6. Save the document on a disk and print it out. Be sure to put the disk and print-out safely in your American Memory folder.

Figure 4–1. Searching the Life Histories Handout

Creating a Found Poem

Once a group had completed reading through the text I gave them a second hand-out (see Figure 4–2) based on the chart we had created earlier and sent them back to the computer lab to compose their poem. It took several class sessions for all groups to complete this process.

Adam, Brent, and Sam Work With the Life Histories Adam, Brent, and Sam worked well together, taking great care to go carefully, step by step, through the process, as I had done. They explored several manuscripts before deciding to use the transcript of Giacomo Coletti, an Italian granite worker. This manuscript was very different from "Noboddy Boddas You." Mary Tomasi, the writer-interviewer, had

---

AMERICAN MEMORY
CREATING A FOUND POEM FROM A LIFE HISTORY MANUSCRIPT

Goal: To craft the immigrant manuscript previously selected into a found poem.

1. Read your selected manuscript. (Do this with your group away from the computer using your print-out).

    Strategies to help:
    Use dictionaries, atlases, and other resources as needed.
    Use context before and after unfamiliar words.
    Work as a group—three heads are better than one!
    Ask a teacher to help.
    Use a highlighter to mark parts that you think will work well in your poem.

2. Create the found poem.

    Return to computer.
    Access your manuscript from American Memory.
    Open a MS Word file.
    Cut and paste selections from your manuscript into your Word file.
    Revise as necessary

    Strategies to help:
    Be sure it sounds like a poem.
    Consider shape, order, line length.
    Take out stuff.
    Think about beginning and ending (framing).

Figure 4–2. Found Poem Handout

chosen to write up the results of her interview in a lyrical third-person account. Far from being daunted by the fact that it was a lengthy text, the boys proudly told me it was ten printed pages, single spaced too! At first I was worried that they would be overwhelmed trying to work their way through so much text. Their reading abilities varied, and this was unfamiliar and very different from the stories they were used to reading. But they had loved creating the poem from "Noboddy Boddas You" and were determined to create one as good from the manuscript they had discovered.

As I wandered around checking in on different groups I would come across Adam, Brent, and Sam highlighters in hand, busily working their way through the text. "You seem to know what you are doing," I commented on one of my visits.

"Oh," said Adam. "We found this part that mentions Nina's warm kitchen and then noticed that there were lots of food names in the manuscript. So we decided our poem would be about food." The boys had divided the pages among themselves and each was highlighting every reference to food.

Once a group had completed a read-through of their manuscript, they returned to the computer, copied the manuscript into a word processing document, and worked on crafting a poem just as we had done all together with "Noboddy Boddas You." Adam, Brent, and Sam were completely involved in their poem. At one point they called me over and asked if a found poem could use letters in new combinations. When I asked why, they explained that they wanted to use the word "love" in their poem but hadn't been able to find it in their manuscript. While I know of no firm rules surrounding found poetry, I made one for them: "only actual words from the text." However, they eventually found the word "love," about which Sam noted, "We had to look through every page carefully for it." They also got other senses such as smell into their final poem. It is a delightful ode to the foods of Giacomo Coletti's homeland.

In Nina's Warm Kitchen

It is pleasant to open the door to
Nina's warm kitchen.
I love to smell
the
strong
black coffee,
slices of salami,
the small Italian buns
that have been oven heated

in Nina's warm kitchen.

A dish of cereal, bowls of soup,
crushed barley or cream soups,
a gallon of our red wine,
vegetables cooked, a tasty stew
in milk.

in Nina's warm kitchen.

pudding,
cottage cheese,
cornmeal slabs with
vegetable salad in its dressing
of olive oil and wine vinegar. Chicken
squares of yellow ravioli are the Sunday
dishes.

in Nina's warm kitchen.

spaghetti piled high macaroni,
tomato sauce and cheese,
a stewed rabbit,
cake and pies

All in Nina's warm kitchen.

Amelia, Olivia, and Lauren Work with the Life Histories Amelia, Olivia, and Lauren (or AOL, as they wrote on their folder) were very enthusiastic when they started to search for a manuscript for their found poem. Olivia, in particular, had been so excited about "Noboddy Boddas You" that she had shown her mother the site at home.

These girls, like the boys, were remarkably comfortable, with the search process. They easily followed the necessary steps to get the list of immigration Life Histories and explored them with enthusiasm. Before long they had selected "William Whytock" for their found poem. This manuscript was produced in Texas and is designated, "Folkstuff" by the writer, Nellie B. Cox. Miss Cox introduces Mr. Whytock briefly and then allows him to tell his own story. This first-person account was much more like the oral histories the girls had done themselves, so their challenge in reading the manuscript was primarily the unfamiliar words, phrases, and information. Olivia was the strongest reader in the group, but together they persevered to make sense of a most intriguing story, carefully highlighting sections of the manuscript they wanted to use for their poem.

Once they completed their reading of the text, they returned to the computer and copied all their highlighted text into a word processing document. Lauren commented later that, "We found some parts that didn't have to do with immigration, like milking the goat and walking on the riverside, but it sounded like a poem." The task to create a poem was a challenging one because, unlike the "In Nina's Warm Kitchen" group, they had not discovered a general theme, such as food, to guide them. Rather, they struggled to decide how to make the narrative flow, what to put in, what to leave out to make it a poem.

After they worked some on their own, I worked with them helping them to recognize sections that focused on immigration themes. This included why Mr. Whytock came to the United States and his experiences making his way into the American heartland. It also, unfortunately, required the girls to eliminate some lively descriptions of ranch life, such as his story of having to help "milk, of all things, a goat. It was a wild creature and I had to hold the goat while Mrs. Hill did the milking." They sensed that Mr. Whytock's description of the "side to side" motion of the boat sounded like a poem and enjoyed the sounds of unfamiliar words like "macadamized" and "pig iron." Finally, they were very concerned with the shape of the poem.

Big Appetite
I was born in the city of Edinburgh, Scotland.
But when the immigration agent
talked to me and five young fellows,
he made the states sound
so fine,
so wonderful,
that
we were in a hurry to start.

The boat on which we came over
was loaded with pig iron
and
as the boat rolled,
the iron shifted from side to side.

Some of the boys were in the beds,
others were playing cards,
when an extra hard lurch sent the ones in bed out on the floor,
the ones on one side slid across to the other.

We came in November, 1884.
The immigration agent took us to San Antonio,
some went on to California.

I had been accustomed to macadamized
streets in my native city and those

streets in San Antonio were so
rough that we held on with
both hands.
All the vehicles
were drawn by mules.

My friend at
Menard had told us that we had better
leave our valuables with him.
I didn't have anything
except a gold watch,
which I had brought from the home country
but I was
glad I had left it,
for the stage was held up.

Being out in the open air and in a new
country
gave me a BIG appetite.

Touring Turn-of-the-Century America: Photographs From the Detroit Publishing Company, 1880–1920 The next stage of the unit was to search a photograph collection for images that would be used in the final collages. We used the Detroit Publishing Company Collection, a massive collection of photographs from the turn of the century. I assumed that the children would find searching for photographs easier than searching for text, but for a number of reasons I turned out to be wrong. For many this was the most challenging part of the unit.

Modeling the Process I began by demonstrating how to search the Detroit Publishing Collection for photographs to illustrate our group poem "Noboddy Boddas You." As before, I used a large monitor with the class facing me. While I had explored the collection previously and had even tried searching for images related to the poem the day before, it turned out that this particular lesson was full of unexpected turns and difficulties. Fortunately, I always feel comfortable making mistakes in front of my students. Kris was there to support me as well as Bill Tally and Lois Kohn-Claar, researchers from the EDC Center for Children and Technology, where the educational side of the American Memory Fellows Program originated. Bill turned out to be incredibly helpful by giving the children an excellent description of the Collection since he had worked with it far more than I had. Kris helped me as I clumsily attempted to save images on the hard drive and Lois provided some superb tips to help the children when they began searching independently.

I showed the children what happened when I searched using the keyword "immigration." We quickly decided that none of the images that resulted from that search would work for the poem. We then tried other keywords: pushcart peddlers, Orchard Street, restaurant, etc. It was much harder than searching the Life Histories. At the end, I had found the following images that I felt might work as illustrations:

- Union Square, New York (keyword: pushcart peddlers)
- Mott Street, New York (keyword: pushcart peddlers)
- Cafe Martin, New York (keyword: restaurants)
- The Ghetto, New York (keyword: Lower East Side)
- Interior of Tenement (keyword: Tenements)
- Italian Neighborhood (keyword: Delancey Street)

After the children started their own searches I completed a collage for "Noboddy Boddas You" so they could see the possibilities and search accordingly. I ended up doing a lot more searching on my own to find images I felt were suitable for the poem. I then cut-up the print-outs, colored them, and manipulated them on the paper along with the text of the poem until it was what I wanted it to be.

I especially wanted the children to be aware that they could use images differently from what they really were. For example, I came across an photo of two men, one giving the other a light for his cigarette. I also found an interior scene complete with a tea kettle. For the collage, I cut the men out of their photo, cut the tea kettle out and reworked the rest so that the kettle sat on a table, as if at Beliska's Restaurant, with the two men apparently on their way in. Above the poem I put a photo of Mott Street, a wonderful street scene which included a restaurant sign. I placed the poem in the middle with the images surrounding it and then colored all the black-and-white photos with colored pencils.

Searching Detroit Publishing At the next session I showed the children the collage I had made to broaden their sense of the possible photographs they might search for. I then reviewed the search process with them. As before we created a chart of strategies for searching this particular collection.

Detroit Publishing Objective/Goal: Find pictures having to do with your found poem (maximum of ten).

Search Strategies:
- Try to use specific keywords: Italian Food.
- Combine words into phrases: e.g., pushcart peddlers.

- Consider word order: e.g., kitchen interiors not interiors kitchen.
- Experiment with different combinations.
- Be careful with plurals: e.g., restaurant not restaurants.
- Use ethnic names: e.g., Italian.
- Use bibliographic information given on the Web pages.
- Use vocabulary from other immigration activities: e.g., immigration, tenement, Ellis Island, Lower East Side, Little Italy, Delancey Street.

I then gave each group a handout (see Figure 4–3). They were required to look through their manuscripts and find ten keywords before going to the computer lab. This, Lois' idea, would help them focus their search and keep it from being too overwhelming.

AMERICAN MEMORY
SEARCHING THE DETROIT PUBLISHING COMPANY

Goal: To find ten photos to use in a collage with your found poem. Remember that your overall objective is to created a final collage that evokes the immigration experience.

1. Planning your search

   Remember how Ms. Edinger searched yesterday using general and specific key words. Below, write down ten words from your immigration studies as well as your manuscript to help you begin your search. Show these to a teacher before going to the computer.

   General Words   **Specific Words**

   1. _____   1. _____

   2. _____   2. _____

   3. _____   3. _____

   4. _____   4. _____

   5. _____   5. _____

2. Try the words in your search. Save each image by holding the mouse down, with the cursor on the image, selecting "Save" from the pop-up menu, and then naming it what it is, e.g., "pushcarts." Print them out if you can. Finally, list them on the back of this page in case you need to find them again.

Figure 4–3. Searching for Photos Handout

Adam, Brent, and Sam Search for Photographs The boys quickly came up with the following key words:

- General Words: food, kitchen, drinks
- Specific Words: Italian food, Italian Kitchen, Red Wine
  (You may note they had six words not ten. But I was kind; I knew they were excited about starting the actual search and allowed them to go.)

I had thought the boys would have an easy time finding images to go with "Nina's Warm Kitchen," but as was often the case during this unit, I was wrong. This was partly because the Detroit Collection did not seem to have a lot of images of food, but also because the boys were very particular as to what they wanted and were unwilling to downgrade their expectations. Rather, they became remarkably tenacious, trying every possible word combination to find what they wanted. "To find our Nina we would type in 'woman'," said Sam, "and it would give us everything. A woman carrying stuff. A woman on the shoulder of a bag and girls and stuff. Brent tried 'female cook' which didn't work and then finally tried 'woman cook,' and that worked." They found each image in their final collage, from the bread to the turkey to the other food, after a great deal of searching.

For their final collage they reworked the poem so that it would go from left to right rather from top to bottom and told me that they enjoyed most coloring it in.

At the end of the unit, as we were reviewing what they had done, Sam told me that he had changed the number of images a search would return from 100 to 200. Thus, when he put a keyword, more images came back. They learned to read the image titles to know which were worth looking at and which weren't. I was amazed at the way they worked on this, with almost no adult help.

Amelia, Olivia, and Lauren Search for Photographs The girls in this group came up with the following words initially as they searched for photos to illustrate their poem, "Big Appetite":

- General Words: food, watch, boat, immigration, farm
- Specific Words: hamburger, pig iron, Scotland, gold watch, card playing

The girls were quite successful in their searches, notably in finding many photographs containing pig iron. However, they decided that the photos of pig iron didn't look like anything so they ended up not using them. "A lot of the boats we looked up were like army boats and they were so little, so we found this one, but when we colored it in it looks so realistic." For their final collages they too cut out images from photos, moved them about along with the poem, and colored them in.

Presentation At the end, each group memorized their poem and presented it to the class. Some did this more successfully than others, but each group was extremely proud of what they had done. Finally, I "published" the poems by putting them on the Web and on a bulletin board outside our room.

What Adam, Brent, and Sam Learned Adam, Sam, and Brent felt that their poem told a lot about the food that Italians brought to this country. After all, noted Sam, pizza didn't originate in New York. They also felt they learned an enormous amount about how to do on-line searches: at one point they changed more photographs by changing the search from 100 to 200.

Asked to comment briefly on what they had learned, the boys wrote as follows:

Sam
1. I learned that not all immigrants stayed in New York City.
2. I learned that each immigrant's life was very different (e.g., they became farmers, workers, poor, etc.)
3. I learned a lot about food.

Brent
1. I learned how foods were brought to the USA.
2. I learned that people immigrated not only to Ellis Island but to other places.

Adam
I learned a lot about how people brought their culture along and how Americans used it. Like pasta, macaroni, rice, etc.

What Amelia, Olivia, and Lauren Learned The girls noted that they hadn't really considered that people went to places beyond Ellis Island. Lauren, a veteran Internet user, felt she had learned to be more specific with the words in her searches, "I didn't know that search engines searched for every word. I learned that you have to be more specific." Olivia felt the picture part was "the most fun part."

Asked what they had learned the girls wrote:

Amelia
I learned that sometimes you immigrate just because someone makes the place sound good. I also learned it can be hard to ride on a boat and when you get to the new country it can turn out good or bad. I never knew people rode on a boat with pig iron.

Lauren
I learned what people did on the boat and what was on the boat. On the boat they played cards and got extra hard lurches.

Olivia

What I learned about immigration is the hardships people had coming to America. I learned that some immigrants came on boats loaded with pig iron. Some immigrants went to work on ranches and in 1864 vehicles were drawn by mules. Some immigrants were made to milk wild goats too.

Final Reflections

I was exhilarated throughout this first experience with Found History. Most likely it was partly due to my frustration with History Firsthand the year before, when the children had seemed so uninspired by the American Memory Collections. I had been so inspired by them, I knew they could be too if I could find the right way. The children were excited about the found poetry and collages from the start. My own happiness stemmed from watching the unit go so well and the children do even more than I had expected.

To me, a successful unit is one I want to do again, and when I do it again I revise it, consider what I saw working and not working with the children, and what they might need or not need to make it better for them. During the year I stay on the lookout for materials that might enhance the unit in any way. When I do it again I'm armed with my experiences of the previous year. The content, concepts, and skills to be learned may be the same, but the learners will not be. And each learner will bring his or her own knowledge and way of learning to the unit.

I recently completed teaching Found History with my 1999–2000 class. It was a marvelous experience. Since a number of children in the class were of West Indian heritage, I decided to use a West Indian Life History for our model poem. The children were as excited and enthusiastic with "Down in the West Indies" as the previous year's class had been with "Noboddy Boddas You." It was interesting to watch the groups search the Life Histories and, in two instances, pick the same manuscripts as last year's class. However, these groups created completely new and different poems with these manuscripts. For the collages I provided more materials, and the result were much more dramatic than the previous year's. My model collage for "Down in the West Indies" contained tissue paper, cloth, and construction paper along with the photographs and the text of the poem. The children's own collages were also much more dramatic. Finally, the children went much further with their presentations. A fifth-grade teacher, Sage Sevilla-Morillo, had a special weekly program in her class called Arts Connection, which included activities that extended text into movement, performance, and even music. My class and I were inspired by a Martin Luther King Day assembly her class did, so I invited her to come to my class to introduce them to some of the Arts Connection techniques. Using "Down in the West Indies," Sage taught my students how to use sound and movement to present the poem in a wonderful new way. The children then worked in their groups to create similar performances with their own poems.

In both years of the Found History Unit, the children showed me that their ability to manage technology was beyond what I had expected. They helped me to recognize that immigration happens all over the United States, not just in New York. They helped me to better appreciate poetry and collage and to want to know more about both. Their enthusiasm fueled mine and helped me to expand the unit into performance, movement, and music. They helped me to see how primary sources can make the study of U.S. immigration new and different. Finally, I learned new things with my students. Pig iron on boats? Never heard of it before. Immigrants on ranches? Somehow I had never associated ranches and cowboys with immigrants. An Italian stew in milk? A brand new idea for me too.

I'm certain to do Found History again next year. I'm also certain that it will be new and different again because of my new discoveries, my students' ideas and interests, and my colleagues. I'm also sure it will be wonderful. Learning always is for me.

Questions & Answers

Q: I've taken a look at the American Memory site and you are right, it is huge! While I'm very intrigued by a number of collections and would love to use them in my teaching, I'm also very intimidated by them. Any suggestions on how to get started?

A: I'm so glad you asked! The Library is very invested in having K–12 teachers use the American Memory collections. The American Memory Fellows Program is only one of many initiatives to help teachers use the materials. Probably the best place to find help is at the Learning Page (http://learning.loc.gov/learn/). This is a Web site explicitly created to help educators and students use American Memory. It includes the following areas:

- *Search Help.* This provides easy access to the collections by way of people, places, and times and topics.
- *Features.* These are interactive essays that focus on topics and themes useful to K–12 audiences. Recent and current features include Elections, Inventors & Inventions, Thanksgiving, and Immigration.
- *Learn More About It.* These are interactive summaries of collections that highlight common historical themes. Searching strategies and sample language arts and social studies activities are provided.
- *Activities.* These are fun exercises for students, such as a Big Picture jigsaw puzzle and an Inventors & Inventions treasure hunt.

- *Lesson Ideas.* This is where History Firsthand resides, along with many other worthwhile lessons using the American Memory collections. Most were created and field-tested by other American Memory Fellows.

Q: I loved your use of found poetry. Can you tell me more about it?

A: Found poetry is evidently a rather recent invention. In searching the Web for information, I discovered plenty of found poetry, but little about its origins. It seems to have developed organically in the sixties. Finding samples of found poetry proved to be difficult. Much as I admire poetry and poets, it is not a genre I read voraciously on my own. So when I began searching for found poems, I wasn't familiar with poets who use the technique. Fortunately, someone mentioned that Annie Dillard did a 1996 collection of found poetry: *Mornings Like This.* I also highly recommend Alison Westfall and Laura Mitchell's "Enhancing a Poetry Unit with American Memory" <http://memory.loc.gov/ammem/ndlpedu/lesson98/poetry/poem.html>, which gave me the idea in the first place.

Q: I would love to explore other ways of using primary sources in creative writing.

A: A wonderful resource for this is Margot Fortunato Galt's (1992) *The Story in History: Writing Your Way into the American Experience.* Galt, who has a doctorate in American Studies, is a poet and experienced writing teacher. This book is full of tried and tested techniques she has used with students at all levels, elementary through college. She begins, as I do, with personal history suggesting ways to write poems about family, names, and other personal data. In other parts of the book she recommends the use of oral histories, photographs, and maps. Galt's focus is very much on writing, although she is also careful to value historical accuracy. Ironically, when I first read this book several years ago while researching my early book on teaching history, I dismissed it as too focused on creative expression and not enough on historical thinking. When I returned to it recently after my work with American Memory and found poetry, I realized that she was much closer to what I was doing than I thought. I have now reread her book several times and feel she offers many exciting ways for students to creatively present history.

A Dream

A dream, a dream of freedom between brothers
A dream, a dream that has been hated by
some, loved by some, awed by all.

A dream

Poems

by Mara

by: Becky

Ballots

Amendment 15:

As long as you are a U.S.A. citizen
nobody shall stop any-
one from voting on
account of race.

Weave a Quilt

Weave a quilt, where black, and
white are woven together.
Weave a quilt of freedom
Weave a quilt of peace
Weave a quilt where black, and
white are woven together.

They Say

They say, they say we are equal
They say, they say we go hand
in hand
They say, they say we have
overcome.

They say, but we know

5

Real Government
Taking On the Constitution

I learned that the Constitution is of big importance. If you look at it right away you will probably say, oh my gosh I don't get it. But see I've read parts of it and know what it's about. So I could easily tell you briefly that it's a set of basic rules that we must follow. Just like any rules except these are much more important. If you did something bad in school you would probably go to the principal. If you break a rule that is in the Constitution which would be considered a law you would probably go to jail or serve a sentence.

One day I was driving to Connecticut with my dad. We were listening to the news on the radio. It was talking about senators. This was the time in school that me and Gordy were working on our article. I asked my dad a question [ending in] ". . . the senators, right?" He answered, yes. And I felt great knowing I knew something.

I learned about impeachment, laws, powers, the Congress. It helped me follow the news, even the ridiculous Monica Lewinsky story. It was wonderful.

How does one teach government to fourth-graders? That was my fourth-grade colleagues and my dilemma some years ago upon being asked to develop and teach a unit on government. All of us had addressed the issue before in different ways. One teacher had created a micro society: after investigating different forms of government, everything from dictatorships to parliamentary systems, his class chose one for themselves. Another had focused on classroom rules and her students had eventually written their own constitution. I had done a simulation many years earlier that enabled my students to understand the importance of democracy. A special law program had provided our students with insights into the justice system, complete with mock trials and field trips to actual courthouses. And all of us had seized every opportunity to use current events to deepen the children's understanding of government. This time, though, we wanted something different, something that would build on the other parts of the curriculum already in place, provide us with a sense of community across the grade, and still be flexible enough to allow for individual teacher styles and passions. After many conversations we reached consensus: Our yearlong theme was citizenship with a focus on immigration. In the course of their studies, our students became very familiar with the process of becoming a U.S. citizen. Thus, it seemed that ending the year with a look at the nature of U.S. citizenship itself would be perfect. And no better vehicle existed for doing so then the Constitution itself. We decided that all of us would begin this final unit with a study of the actual document, and then each class would explore the amendments in ways most related to our own individual styles and passions.

Intrigued, I went to work. First of all, how on earth was I going to teach the Constitution to nine-year-olds? I went into my files and found plenty: copy after copy of the Constitution, special unit materials from the Constitution's Bicentennial celebration, reproducible workbooks, information from the League of Women Voters and other civic organizations, even an old textbook-based unit I had created years ago. Over the years I had accumulated all of this material from a variety of sources. Some came directly from the League of Woman Voters and the National Archives where the Constitution is housed. Other materials were designed more specifically for schools—blackline masters and workbooks, many of which are still available from Social Studies School Services (<http://socialstudies.com>). With old purple dittos full of questions about ratification, dreary blackline masters on checks and balances, and fake-old copies of the Constitution strewn about me, I decided to read the Constitution itself. And what a revelation that was. This is an extraordinary document, I thought: How incredible to think that after so many years it still works as well as it does. Reading it again, I began to wonder how I could help my students experience the same sense of awe.

I went to visit a former colleague, Tom Doran, now teaching at another school. He and his fifth graders spent the year studying democracy in ancient Greece and in the United States. I was especially interested in the materials he used for the United States portion of the curriculum. We had taught closely for years and I knew that his materials would be age-appropriate and useful at creating engaging and authentic learning experiences. Tom enthusiastically pulled out the materials he used to teach the Constitution. One caught my eye, Channing E. Bete Co., *About the Constitution of the United States: We the People* (1980), an annotated Constitution for kids. I was intrigued. Annotating was already familiar to my students. Looking through the booklet I became ever more enthusiastic. It was very child-friendly, clearly designed, and full of little cartoonlike drawings to illustrate particularly difficult points; it provided simple definitions of difficult words and many explanations in simple language to support child-readers. Why not have the children read this? I thought. They could use the annotations already in the booklet and add more of their own.

Of course, reading and annotating the Constitution were going to be quite different from my students' previous experiences with annotation. So far, they had only used the technique with narratives. I introduced annotating in September with *Charlotte's Web*. After observing me read and annotate a chapter by searching for underlying themes, literary devices such as foreshadowing, wonderful words, and references to White's own life, the children did the same, each creating a unique personal copy of *Charlotte's Web*. (for more about this unit please refer to the chapter on E. B. White in my book *Fantasy Literature in the Classroom*). During our study of the Pilgrims, the children worked in groups reading and annotating excerpts from *Mourt's Relation*. With this firsthand account, the children focused on making sense of the antiquated language and sentence structure. Both *Charlotte's Web* and *Mourt's Relation* were narratives; the Constitution was certainly not. My students would need to use their previously developed reading and annotating skills in a new and different way. No doubt some may wonder if I was being realistic. These were nine- and ten-year-olds after all. And even adults find reading the Constitution a challenge. However, somehow I just knew my kids would be able to do it and enjoy it as well. *Mourt's Relation* had been challenging too, yet they had navigated it with great success. I knew that they would relish the idea of attacking the Constitution itself. It was the real thing, and they always preferred the real story, the real document, over abridgments and summaries.

Once I had decided to have the children read the Constitution, I had to think of a way to do so that would be intriguing and meaningful to them. As I was mulling over this problem, my director mentioned that a parent had asked if a study of the states was in the school's curriculum. Did they ever learn the names of all the states and where they were located? this parent wanted to know. My director quite honestly had to acknowledge that we did not have that built into our curriculum. While she did not then insist that I immediately develop a states unit, I began thinking about why it might be important to do so. While many educators joke about the irrelevance of state reports, I wasn't so sure I agreed with them. My students lived in New York City and many had very little sense of the country beyond the city limits. Their knowledge of the rest of the country was pretty eclectic: they knew most of the other states because of their sports teams or as vacation destinations. I decided that I wanted them to know about the rest of the country and that a states unit might be just the way to do that. I began to think about how I could create a project that would combine the children's work with the Constitution and learning something about the states. The result was the *United States of America Quilt Project*.

I have taught this unit for four years. It has varied depending on children's interests, current events, colleagues, and special opportunities; however, the over-arching structure has remained consistent each year.

Introduction
The States
- Research about different states and making patches for the quilt.
- Basic mapping and spelling skills as to where the different states are located and how their names are spelled.

The Constitution
- Events leading up to its creation.
- Reading, annotating, and understanding the Constitution.
- The Bill of Rights and Amendments.
- Living Constitution Project.

Introduction

When beginning the unit I ask the children to consider what our country's name, "The United States of America," actually means. Invariably certain students, sufficiently knowledgeable about U.S. history, are able to explain that we are a collection of states as well as one nation on the American continent, and that is the explanation of this name. From this I segue into a description of the project: the creation of a story quilt of the United States on the back bulletin board of our classroom. The center of the quilt always has fifty patches representing all fifty states, while other parts of the quilt are about the Constitution, the Bill of Rights, and the Amendments. And although I have done proper cloth quilts filled with batting in the past, this particular quilt has always been a paper one (much easier, frankly, to do!).

The States

The children work individually and in pairs to create patches for each of the fifty states. They have great fun with this assignment. I provide them with a data sheets for tracking down basic information about their selected states. I have heard and read complaints about the tediousness of state research projects, but my students have always found it great fun. They are intrigued by the accumulation of facts: annual rainfall, highest elevation, state bird, state motto, state flag, and so forth. I press them to find the highlights of the state's history, which fascinates them as well. And the research is certainly easy to do. Much they can find in my old classroom encyclopedia, in books on the different states in our school library, on the Internet at home and at school, and in CD encyclopedias such as Encarta. Once they have completed the data sheet, I provide them with specially sized paper (so that all fifty states fit on the board) for the quilt square. They select whatever they wish to highlight from their research to put on this patch, which becomes the center of our United States of America story quilt (see the example in Figure 5–1).

On a more pedestrian note, the children are also required to learn the location and spelling of all fifty states. We do a variety of activities to solidify basic geography skills, such as being able to say which state boarders another on its southeastern side, and similar information. In weekly quizzes, each child is given a map of the United States and has to accurately write in a predetermined set of states. Week one consists of the eastern states, week two the central states, and week three the western states. For week four the children are challenged to put all fifty states in their rightful locations. And spelling counts! While I don't expect that the children will remember every spelling or every location, I do think they will have a far better sense of where the states are located. No more cases, I hope, of these New York City-centric children considering Illinois a western state or having absolutely no idea where North Dakota is.

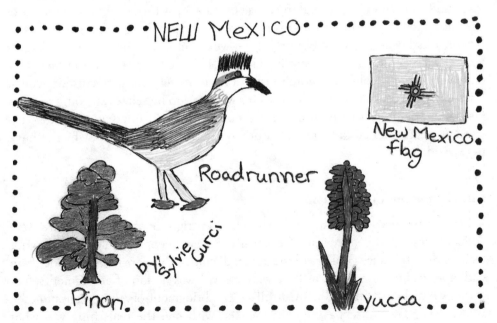

Figure 5–1. Sylvie's State Patch

I must admit, I don't require that they learn the state capitals as well. While I see good reasons to know where the states are geographically and how to spell their names correctly, I am not aware of similar reasons for knowing the capitals. Recently a student who had, on his own, memorized the state capitals, proudly asked me if I knew the capital of Missouri. Having lived in St. Louis and remembering a trip to the state capital in eighth grade, I said that I was certain that it was Kansas City. Absolutely not, he told me. It was Jefferson City. Certain that my memory couldn't be that faulty, I checked an atlas, at which point I had to concede that school trip must have been to Jefferson City, not Kansas City, as I'd long thought. Now I do indeed finally have it right: the capital of Missouri is Jefferson City. Remarkably, though, I've never needed that information until now. As a result, the only state capital my students *have* to know is Albany, the capital of their own state, New York.

The Constitution

The state patches are great fun for the children to do, but the heart of the unit has always been our work with the Constitution. In 1999, after several years of having children read, annotate, and summarize sections of the Constitution, I decided to try something a bit different. In previous years the children had been remarkably successful in their efforts at making sense of the Constitution. At the same time, the annotated Constitution for kids I had been using no longer seemed quite sufficient. I had been so excited to find it: However, after having used it for several years, I was beginning to feel that it was tired. I wanted one that was more up-to-date, with more vocabulary, more illustrations, more references to current events. For some time I considered creating such a publication myself, even going so far as discussing the project with an interested publisher. Then I had a better idea. Instead of creating a new kid-friendly annotated Constitution myself, why not have my class do it?

Introducing the Constitution

When I introduced the unit, I told the children right at the start that we were going to create a kids' annotated Constitution. Many people, I told them, did not feel children their age could read the actual document, preferring to provide them with abridged versions. But, as they well knew, I was no fan of abridgments. Together we had laughed at Lewis Carroll's own abridgment of *Alice's Adventures in Wonderland, The Nursery Alice*. They agreed with me, the real thing was what we all wanted. My students were terribly excited by the idea of creating a kid-annotated Constitution, one for their peers, not for grown-ups. The idea that there were those who felt they were too young to do it made the challenge all the more attractive. They had been annotating hard stuff all year: *Charlotte's Web*, *Mourt's Relation*, . . . If I thought they could do it, then they thought they could too. Their enthusiasm was great to see, and they would need it to delve into this challenging project.

That being settled, we moved into the unit and a discussion of what they already knew about the Constitution.

The Constitution

What we know about it. May 26, 1999

> AMELIA: It is the government and is in Washington, D.C.
> PAUL: It is the laws of the USA.
> SARAH W.: If the government wants to do something, they look to the Constitution to see if they can.
> BRENT: It is a document with laws that every state follows.
> LAUREN: It has something to do with the President, the government and "those people."
> SAM: [It has] something about impeaching the President.
> ADAM: How to do it is in the Constitution.
> KATHARINE: It is old.
> OLIVIA: Free country and no kings.
> MICHAEL: One of the two most important U.S. documents and has something to do with civil rights.

I began by orienting the children chronologically. I pointed out that the events leading up to the writing and adoption of the Constitution occurred over one hundred and fifty years after the Mayflower voyage, the historical event with which they were most familiar. I next read aloud Betsy and Giulio Maestro's (1987) *A More Perfect Union: The Story of the Constitution*. As I read it I annotated it orally, especially with certain basic facts about the Revolution and why it occurred. I was not teaching a chronological U.S. history course, so the children did need some background in the events leading up to the Constitution's writing. However, they knew something of colonial America from the Pilgrims and had certainly heard of the Revolution. They took notes while I did this.

Sam's Notes on U.S. Constitution Background
1627–Plimoth Plantation
(big gap to indicate passage of time)

1776 King George and the Declaration of Independence
13 colonies fought Revolutionary War to win freedom from England.

Each state [afterwards] had own government.

No cooperation. No president.

Each state sent a delegation to convention in Philadelphia.

Discussed many plans. Eventually decided on compromise.

Many drafts.

New Constitution.

Signed by 39 delegates on Sept. 17, 1787.

simple majority [of states] needed [to ratify]

June 21 New Hampshire [last state needed to ratify] said yes

For homework the children used these notes to write a summary of the story of the Constitution. The next day they used their notes and summaries and we created the following whole-class overview of the Constitution's history.

Constitution

Background and Overview

In 1776 the people in the British colonies were getting mad. These thirteen colonies had been reasonably content for over one hundred years. However, things started changing. For example, the colonists had to pay taxes that helped England not themselves. Well known ones included the Stamp Tax and the Tea Tax. Eventually, the colonists became outraged resulting in the Declaration of Independence.

After the Revolutionary War the thirteen colonies started a new government. However, there were problems. Each state (former colony) had their own money, government rules, stamps, etc. They did not cooperate very well, had no money, and had no general leader like a President. In 1787 they decided to have a convention in Philadelphia to fix things.

James Madison became the official note taker and George Washington was elected leader. They made up rules of conduct so they wouldn't fight. They discussed a lot of different plans. The Virginia Plan was for a brand new government. It was to be a government elected by "the people" in three parts: a president, a congress, and a court system. Some delegates were surprised, but eventually they voted to create a new government. Now they considered the Virginia Plan in detail. A big problem was the smaller states felt they didn't get as much representation as the bigger states. So representatives of the smaller states came up with the New Jersey Plan which was similar to the old government. Most important was that the states were treated the same regardless of size.

Finally after much debate and discussion a new plan called the Connecticut Compromise was worked out. It included parts of the Virginia Plan, the New Jersey Plan, and some new ideas as well.

On Monday, Sept. 17, 1787, 39 delegates signed the new Constitution. Then they returned to the states. Nine had to approve it (two-thirds majority) for it to go into effect. On June 21, 1788 New Hampshire voted yes—the ninth state. So on July 4, 1799, there were big celebrations for the new government.

George Washington was elected president, a Congress elected, and courts set up. Soon after, the Bill of Rights (first ten amendments) was written.

With this background solidly in place, we were now ready to take on the Constitution itself!

A First Look

We began as I did every year with the Channing E. Bete Co. annotated Constitution: *About the Constitution of the United States: We the People*. While I do consider it dated, it is still the best vehicle I have found for providing my students with direct contact with the Constitution. As described earlier (see p. 92), it is a simple, inexpensive booklet with the whole Constitution nicely and clearly laid out, supplemented with ample annotations, cartoons, and other structures to help the children make sense of the document directly. Each child receives a copy to mark up and use. To help them gain some sense of the document, my first activity involves simply looking through the whole booklet to get some sense of what it is, what the parts are, and how to use the booklet. The booklet is clearly produced: the Constitution is on one side of the page and the annotations in large red and gray bubbles alongside it. Sections that have been amended are clearly crossed out and, in addition to definitions and information, many of the annotations include simple line drawings. I had the children look at the index and played a simple game to help familiarize them with the different parts of the document. I asked questions like "What page has the Bill of Rights?," "In what article can I find out how to amend the Constitution?," "Which article includes information about citizenship rights?," "What page has information about Congress?," and "How many sections are in Article II?" This helps the children get a sense of the whole document and the way it is organized.

Modeling How to Annotate

With earlier classes my focus was on summarizing, but for this class the focus was on creating a kid-annotated version. This, I decided, would be done as large posters that would go above our state quilt. I found a good version of the Constitution at the National Archives Web site, downloaded it, reworked the font to a size manageable for a poster, and printed it out. For the modeling session, I pasted the Preamble onto a large piece of chart paper with plenty of empty space around it for annotations. I then modeled how I would annotate it as I had done in previous years with other articles. I looked for words I didn't know, looked them up in the dictionary, and then wrote the definitions clearly in red marker next to the underlined word in question.

We, the People of the United States,

in Order to form a *more* (a better government than previous under the Articles of Confederation)

perfect Union, establish *Justice* (fairness),

insure domestic Tranquillity (make sure the country is at peace),

provide for the common *defense* (army),

promote the general *Welfare* (people live well),

and secure the *Blessings of Liberty* (reference to the ideals of the Declaration of Independence)

to ourselves and our *Posterity* (children)

do *ordain* (order)

and establish this Constitution for the United States of America.

A Constitution Glossary

As we discussed the Constitution we were constantly grappling with new vocabulary. Soon we created a glossary on another piece of chart paper and posted it for all to use.

Constitution Glossary
- delegate: representative (from a state)
- compromise: agreement reached when opposing sides give up some of their demands
- ratified (ratify, ratification): the process of voting to approve
- amendments; changes/additions to Constitution
- convention: large gathering of people who have similar interests
- adopted: to approve officially
- unanimous: agreed to by everyone
- popular sovereignty: leader chosen by the people
- federal: several states united and controlled by central government
- Branches of government:
    - Executive: President, Vice President, Cabinet
    - Legislative: Congress makes laws (House of Representatives and Senate)
    - Judicial: System of courts, judges

Children Annotating the Constitution

When it came time for the children to begin their own annotating, I carefully put them into groups to work on the different articles. Each group would annotate a particular article and then present it to the class. This way all would have the experience of closely reading and annotating one part of the Constitution and also learn about the whole. I placed the more advanced readers and tenacious person-

100

alities (who would not give up easily) with the more challenging articles (especially Article I). Finally, before sending them off to work, the children and I created the following chart to remind them of their task and the strategies to achieve it.

Annotating the Constitution

Tasks
1. Annotate (words only) in red booklet assigned article(s).
2. Make poster of article(s) annotated (include pictures and photographs for this).
3. Make final version to be published for other teachers to use with their students. (We ran out of time and did not do this.)
4. Present your article(s) to the class.

Strategies
1. Words I don't know. Mark them.
2. Use bubbles (annotations) in red book and simplified Constitution packet.
3. Use context (read on).
4. If you know a definition, still check it because it may not be the right one (there can be more than one definition), e.g. *domestic* and *ordain*.
5. Check all definitions in dictionaries (for children and adults) until you find one that works in the Constitution.
6. Use class glossary chart.
7. Take turns reading aloud and then put into own words—out loud.
8. Maybe use other books (about the Constitution) and Web pages to help.

Each group began by carefully reading, annotating, and making sense of their particular article using the commercial annotated booklet. To help them, I also gave them an abridged version created by Tarry Lindquist (1997) and available in *Ways That Work: Putting Social Studies Standards into Practice*. Reading this before delving into the real article helped some of the less confident readers. Once I felt that a particular group had thoroughly annotated and understood their section, I gave them the enlarged printed-out version of their article, which they pasted onto chart paper as I'd done with the Preamble. Then they carefully annotated it for their peers. They went far beyond simply defining difficult words and rephrasing the text in simpler language, adding images and historical information that they felt would make their article more real to other children like themselves.

The Article I Group Recognizing that Article I would probably be the most challenging, I assigned the largest group of children to it, seven in all. Addition, I selected students I thought were disciplined and hardworking, and who had proven in previous projects to work well in groups. However, their cooperative natures failed them more than once in this ambitious project. The group quickly divided into two subgroups: boys and girls. The boys worked comfortably with the sections they were responsible for, while the girls, initially far less engaged, struggled to remain focused. Problems arose when the boys who had stayed on task completed their annotations while the girls had not. Eventually, after several contentious sessions, the group successfully completed the annotations. The next step, of greater interest to the girls, was creating their annotated charts. They pasted their copies of the article onto chart paper and used different color markers to highlight words they had defined in their annotations on the side. In several cases they added drawings to further clarify a particular phrase or word. For example, there are several references to the census, and in one case they added a drawing of a "man taking a census." In another case they illustrated "Each House may determine the Rules of its Proceedings, punish its Members for disorderly Behavior, and, with the Concurrence of two thirds, expel a Member" with a drawing of a man announcing to another with a bottle, "Get out, you're drunk," with the caption, "These Rules are Only for the Congress." A king with an X drawn over him illustrated Section 9, with its statement that there be no sort of nobility whatsoever. Amusingly, this group was especially intrigued by the importance of the Treasury and one child spent a very long time drawing a sample counterfeit bill to illustrate Section 10.

The Article II Group A smaller group of four took on Article II, about the executive branch, with alacrity. Katharine, Kenwan, Zain, and Sarah worked seriously, first annotating and being sure they understood the article as presented in both Tarry Lindquist's abridgment and in the booklet. Once they had completed this, they began the work of creating their kid-annotated poster of Article II. At the very top of the poster, in large letters, they wrote: "They wanted a president not a king." This group of children really understood the dramatic shift that the creation of a presidential office meant for people recently under the power of an unjust king. To reinforce the point, below this statement is a portrait of King George III crossed out with "NO KING!" written next to it.

In beginning to discuss just how they would create their kid-annotated Constitution, I had suggested that, in addition to definitions and other pieces of writing, they might want to add images, even, I blithely suggested, visuals from the Internet. At the time I made the suggestion I had absolutely no idea where these images might be found. I suppose I had some vague idea of a clip-art site somewhere that might be useful. However, this group had a far better idea. They went straight for American Memory, the Library of Congress Web site they had used months earlier in their immigration-based projects (see Chapter 4). It had never occurred to me that they might return to American Memory for this project, but they did, and I was delighted. It proved, more than I had thought possible, that they had truly absorbed the search skills presented in the earlier unit.

They found their portrait of King George in an American Memory collection of presidential portraits. To impress upon the viewer the importance of the executive branch, they scattered several portraits of George Washington in the text. In the section on the oath the president must swear when assuming office, they placed a photograph of Franklin Roosevelt being sworn in. (Zain was a rabid Roosevelt enthusiast.) In the section on impeachment three presidents are displayed. First there is Bill Clinton with the caption, "He was impeached." Nearby is Richard Nixon with the caption, "They were ready to impeach him, but he resigned." Finally there is Andrew Jackson above a large lithograph of his trial. Their knowledge of impeachment was greater than any previous class due to Clinton's impeachment and trial a few months earlier. I had expected that they would be fascinated by the sections on impeachment, but it seemed already far in the past to them. Other, less familiar rules, were actually more interesting to them.

My favorite image is a collage constructed by Katharine to illustrate "No person except a natural born citizen, or a citizen of the United States, at the time of the adoption of this Constitution, shall be eligible to the Office of the President." Katharine found a painting of a child and an image of an American flag in one of the American Memory collections, placed the flag in the child's hands and colored them both (see Figure 5–2). Below is her caption, "Someone born in the USA." I especially liked the fact that the child seems to be female. While the Constitution does not explicitly state that only men can become president, it is now more possible for women, something Katharine intended to have her peers, the ultimate audience of this poster, consider.

Throughout, the children carefully circled words they thought might cause their peers difficulties and provided definitions nearby. Thus we have "additional pay" for *emolument*, "salary" for *compensation*, "bad" for *inferior*, and "easy and fastest way" for *expedient*.

Katharine, Zain, Kenwan, and Sarah's annotations indicate their own sure understanding of much in this article and of what their peers would need in order to understand.

Summarizing Articles

An alternative to producing large kid-annotated posters is to have the children summarize articles, as previous classes did. These summaries eventually became borders for our story quilt. After watching me model how to annotate and summarize an article, the children did so themselves. I was quite awed by the tenacity with which they worked on this difficult task. The first year of the unit I hadn't

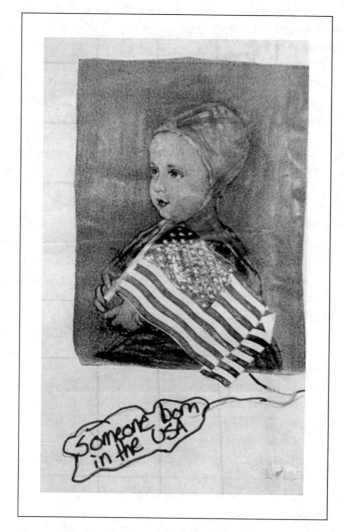

Figure 5–2. Katharine's Visual Annotation

been so sure it was really something fourth graders could manage. While my teacher instincts said they could, I still wondered if I wasn't being overly optimistic about their abilities. Perhaps nine- and ten-year-olds were just not developmentally ready to handle something this abstract and obtuse. However, they were delighted by the challenge and succeeded beyond anything I had expected. Watching the next two classes also do so well was in part the reason I decided to try something different with the following class. Here is Becky and Will's 1998 summary of Article II, Sections 2, 3, and 4:

> The President is commander in chief of the Army and Navy, also of the militia of all the 50 states. When disaster strikes such as riots or some kind of fight the president has the choice to call the National Guard to defend and help the victims.
>
> The President has the power to make treaties with other states or nations. Two thirds of the Senate have to agree with the treaty to make it happen. The President can also fill in empty positions in the Senate by appointing people.
>
> The President must give a State of the Union speech every once in a while to tell his country how they are doing. If something unusual occurs the President can meet with his cabinet and discuss it with them at any time.
>
> The President and Vice President may be removed from office for conviction of bribery, treason, or other high crimes.

Final Presentations and Assessment

Every year, I have the children present their work to the class. Each pair or group has become an expert on one section of the document and is able to teach the class about it. It is remarkable how informed they become about their particular section, not only presenting it but answering questions about it as well. The children are also fascinated by the parts of the Constitution they didn't cover, especially when these relate to their own part or to something they have heard on the news. One year, after these presentations, I asked the children to write down something of what they had learned through their own efforts and from listening to their peers. Some of their comments open this chapter. Here are a few more:

> From my own section I learned about how elections are held. It's not just going in a booth and pulling a lever any more. I had no clue about the U.S. electoral college either. And now when I talk about it I get to hear all the interesting opinions of the law.
> Emily

> I think I learned a lot from my work. My sections were 9 and 10, powers forbidden to Congress and powers forbidden to the states. In those two sections it told me that no kings and queens were allowed and told me that Congress could not do anything about slavery till the year 1808 and many other things like that.
> Bartholt

> I have learned how they would count people for a census like they would count the black slaves as three fifths. I also learned that you have to be 27 or older if you want to be a representative, you must have been a citizen for at least seven years or born here, you must live in the state your represent.
> Wende

I learned that there are so many things that you aren't allowed to do in this country. I also learned there are three branches of government: legislative, executive, judicial. I learned from listening today that the amount of representatives is based on the population of the state.

Evan

I learned that there are 100 senators (2 from each state) in the United States of America. Senators have to be at least 25 years old or they can't run for the Senate. They also have to live in the state where they are working for. I also learned about the Congress can make money and decide how much it is worth. I also learned that the President has to be born in the United States. This unit was really great!

Will

The Bill of Rights and Amendments

After completing our work with the Constitution we always move on to the Bill of Rights and Amendments. For the first three years of the unit each child selected one or two amendments to illustrate. These small illustrations completed our story quilt by bordering it on the top. Illustrating the amendments was an interesting exercise. Some were relatively easy to do, but many were difficult. The children enjoyed learning about Prohibition, for example. In the more abstract cases I suggested the children simply write them, rather than attempting to illustrate them (see, for example, Figure 5–3).

Living Constitution Project

The unit ends every year with an activity or project related to how the Constitution is still meaningful today and in recent history. While I am a big believer in my fourth graders' capacity to grapple with the abstract language and ideas in the Constitution and Amendments, and I know they enjoy learning the story of its creation, I also believe that it is critical to follow up such work with experiences that show the Constitution at work, as a living document that is meaningful in our lives today. After all, our original charge was for the fourth graders to learn about the U.S. government. In order to truly appreciate the Constitution, therefore, they need to have a sense of how it works in reality, to connect it with some contemporary issue that is meaningful to them. Every year this final piece of the unit has been different, depending on current events, the interests and needs of each class, and unexpected opportunities.

The Child's Right to a Home Amendment

The first year I taught the unit there was a great deal of media attention on the plight of homeless children. Many of my students, however, had spent most of the

Figure 5–3. Chessie's Tenth Amendment

year very preoccupied with themselves. We had spent a lot of time on classroom dynamics and interpersonal skills. The issue of rights had been very important to them all year, but in terms of *their* rights within the classroom, *their* rights among their peers, *their* rights as students. It was time, I felt, to move them outside their own world, to consider the rights of children living in very different circumstances. Thus, I decided that our final project would focus on homeless children.

I began by reading aloud several nonfiction picture books about homeless children and Jerry Spinelli's Newbery Award winning book, *Maniac Magee,* the story of a homeless child. These books shocked and disturbed my upper middle class students. Until then they had thought of homelessness exclusively in terms of the often mentally ill homeless adults they saw on the streets every day. They hadn't realized that children could be homeless and immediately wanted to do something about it. I told them that one of the amazing things about the Constitution was that any citizen could propose an amendment. Would they be interested in proposing one for homeless children? I asked. Yes, they responded with great enthusiasm.

With their interest and commitment assured, I told them that we would need to begin by finding out how amendments were proposed and became part of the Constitution. We did this by exploring the recent efforts toward, and ultimate failure of, the ratification of the Equal Rights Amendment. The arguments for and against this particular amendment were relatively easy for the children to comprehend. At first they could see no reason for anyone to object to it until I mentioned that some had feared it would result in unisex bathrooms. That they understood! This investigation helped us to understand the language of proposed amendments and the process that would led to its adoption.

In the course of several conversations about homelessness and exactly what "home" meant, we generated the following:
Home for our class means:

- a real place
- warmth
- permanence
- a place one is used to
- an address
- a place where you don't have to knock
- support
- a place where you can always go
- family
- comfort

Then the class began crafting the proposed amendment itself. Every word was carefully considered, debated, and voted on. For example, the final proposed amendment is explicit about children "under the age of 21." We discussed at length when one became a grown-up. My students were already well aware that one could marry in certain states at much younger ages, and of the lower voting age and the age at which one could serve in the armed forces. However, they decided that it was crucial to protect children as long as possible and picked the age at which one became financially independent as endpoint for the period when all children would be assured of a home. Another discussion revolved around citizenship. Finally, the children decided that being a citizen of the United States didn't matter; that all children on United States soil should have shelter. Others wanted to put in more specifics about how homes would be provided, but I suggested that this would have to be worked out through other laws at both the federal and state level. After much effort they completed their proposed Amendment 28:

Child's Right to a Home Amendment
No child living in the United States, under the age of 21, shall be homeless.

The children then worked in committees to promote the amendment. One group made a video about homeless children in America. Another group wrote letters to our congressional representatives and senators (see Figure 5–4, p. 110). A third group made posters. By the end of the year these previously very self-involved children had not only become far more sensitive to the complicated issues of homelessness, but they had also learned a great deal about the process of government in the United States.

Civil and Human Rights

For the next two years our final projects involved an exploration of human and civil rights. I began this project by providing some background on the Civil Rights Movement. I then read aloud Christopher Paul Curtis' *The Watsons Go to Birmingham—1963*, a powerful work of historical fiction that provides a warm and humorous view of one family and its response to one terrible event of the civil rights period. I also used Casey King and Linda Barrett Osborne's (1997) *Oh, Freedom! Kids Talk About the Civil Rights Movement with the People Who Made It Happen*, which connected nicely to my own students work with oral histories. After some general immersion, the children went off to do their own investigations. One year they worked in groups to research several civil and human rights heroes, such as Martin Luther King, Jr., Nelson Mandela, and Mahatma Gandhi, and presented the results of their research on video. Another year, after the initial immersion in the civil rights period, we looked at some of the powerful poetry written about the movement and the children then wrote and performed poems of their own. In each case, the children were able to connect their hard work in making sense of the Constitution with recent history, current events, and heroic individuals.

1999 Proposed Amendments

With the 1999 class, after all our successful work creating a kid-annotated Constitution, I also wanted to try something new with the amendments. Remembering

CAROLYN B. MALONEY
14TH DISTRICT, NEW YORK

1504 LONGWORTH BUILDING
WASHINGTON, DC 20515–3214
(202) 225–7944

COMMITTEE ON BANKING AND
FINANCIAL SERVICES

COMMITTEE ON GOVERNMENT
REFORM AND OVERSIGHT

DISTRICT OFFICES:

☐ 110 EAST 59TH STREET
2ND FLOOR
NEW YORK, NY 10022
(212) 832–6531

☐ 28–11 ASTORIA BLVD.
ASTORIA, NY 11102
(718) 932–1804

☐ 619 LORIMER STREET
BROOKLYN, NY 11211
(718) 349–1260

Congress of the United States
House of Representatives
Washington, DC 20515–3214

May 29, 1996

Edinger House
The Dalton School
108 East 89th Street
New York, New York 10128

Dear Friends:

Thank you for writing to me to express your concern about America's children. I applaud your interest in this important issue and I am pleased that you have given me the opportunity to share my thoughts with you.

Like you, I believe that children are this country's greatest resource. Throughout my entire career both on the New York City Council and the U.S. Congress, I have fought for the rights of children. In fact, I was the first woman in the City Council's history to give birth while in office.

I am also very concerned about the problem of homelessness. While homelessness is unfortunate under any circumstances, it is particularly tragic when children and their families are forced to live on the street. As a member of the House Banking Committee, I have worked hard to promote legislation aimed at proving a warm and safe home for every American in an effort to eliminate the problem of homelessness once and for all.

Your proposal to protect children by amending the Constitution is an intriguing idea, the premise of which, I agree with. Although it is difficult to amendment the Constitution, I encourage you to continuing working for the goals you believe in and stay involved with the political process.

Once again, thank you for taking the time to contact me. Please do not hesitate to contact me about any issue of mutual concern and keep me informed about your progress on this project.

Sincerely,

CAROLYN B. MALONEY
Member of Congress

CBM/gcg

Figure 5–4. Regarding Our Proposed Amendment

the interest in the failed Equal Rights Amendment, I decided to see what I could find on the Internet about proposed amendments. I was delighted to discover that there was quite a lot. Not only did I learn a great deal more about the ERA, but also about other attempts to amend the Constitution. At the National Organization for Women Web site <http://www.now.org> I learned much more about the

Equal Rights Amendment and the failed efforts to ratify it in 1982. At another site <www.constitutionfacts.com> I found a list of amendments proposed and never adopted. Some included an 1893 attempt to abolish the U.S. Army and Navy, an 1893 attempt to rename the country, "the United States of Earth," a 1924 effort to limit child labor, and more recent efforts to ban flag desecration. The most interesting site I discovered was that of The Banneker Center for Economic Justice, which invites visitors to provide their own proposed amendments <www.progress.org/~banneker/cgibin/ments.html>. Visitors have proposed amendments for religious freedom, to repeal the Sixteenth Amendment, to abolish all laws criminalizing drug use, to ban private ownership, to refrain from undermining the family, and many others.

I was so intrigued by the proposed amendments on the Internet, that I wondered if my students would be equally intrigued. I showed them some of the proposed amendments and suggest that they too propose an amendment. They loved the idea, so I took it even farther by challenging them to make them as much like the amendments already in existence as possible. Given how much time they had already spent reading and making sense of the Constitution, my students had absorbed a remarkable amount of vocabulary and sentence structure, which is reflected in these proposed amendments.

When I began our study of the Constitution that year, I had been certain that of greatest interest would be impeachment; after all, this was only a few months after President Clinton's impeachment. However, this turned out to be far less important to my students than something more worrisome to them: the Columbine shootings. We talked about them, and I wanted my students to feel safe in school. However, I discovered that they had a greater impact than I had realized when my students handed in their proposed amendments. Many were a direct outgrowth of their feelings about the Columbine shootings as well as other seemingly random acts of violence involving guns.

Some of their proposed amendments included:

Changing the Second Amendment
No individual person shall have the right to be armed at any time or place. The only people who have the power to be armed are the U.S. Army and any police in any state. The people who have the power to use weapons may only use them in the case of real emergencies like war and defense. No person should be able to shoot anyone or anything (like animals) for any reasons whatsoever.
Emma

My Amendment
Any U.S. citizen of 21 years of age or older shall not be denied by the U.S. government to vote for president, vice president or any other office.

My Reasons

I think that 21 is a good age for people to be allowed to vote because when you are older you pay more attention to politics so you know more about what's going on. Also since you don't have to vote *most* 18 years olds do not really care who's in office so they don't vote. IF you make it that people have to be older to vote you will get more votes because when *most* people are older they care more about whom is in office.

Sarah W.

The 22nd Amendment

The 22nd Amendment is about presidential term limits. It says that the President of the United States may not be elected more than twice. This was initiated after Franklin D. Roosevelt was elected four times.

I think the 22nd amendment should be abolished. The President should be allowed to be elected more than twice, because if he gets elected and wins that means he is a better candidate than the opposing person. I think the citizens of the United States should decide who's in office.

Bennett

Reflections on Children, Government, and Learning

I've learned many things over the years I've taught this unit:

- That with high yet reasonable expectations and plenty of modeling and help, children can take on the reading of an unabridged section of the Constitution.
- That this unit has become a powerful place to consider current events.
- That issues of rights and responsibilities, always important to us at any age, become highlighted in such a unit.
- That children can surprise me with their learning and thinking in this unit in powerful ways.

Questions & Answers

Q: This seems an ambitious approach for fourth graders. You, no doubt, have a fairly small class size. How do suggest doing such a unit with a much larger class or with multiple sections of students (as is typical in middle school)?

A: I do admit that my class size is usually no more than twenty, and I work with one group of children. If I had a larger class I would probably divide the articles up and make more groups. I discovered that groups larger than four tend to struggle too much with group dynamics. When I had one group of seven annotating Article I, they had a hard time figuring out how to work together. All the smaller groups, even when they squabbled, had an easier time working out problems than did this large group. I probably would also have the kids more involved in the group design. In the past I've done this in different ways, depending on the class. Sometimes I've asked each child to give me a list of ten children (or even more if necessary) he or she could work with in a group. I would then make up the groups using these lists. While time consuming, it was worth it, as the children felt they had input in the groups and worked harder to keep them functioning as a result. Another technique I've used in rearranging seating might also work to make groups (although I admit I have not used it this way). That is to invite children to propose ways of grouping the whole class. I've done this once or twice for seating when I've been unhappy with it. My classroom is arranged like many upper elementary classrooms with desks in groupings of four, five, and six. The children may work in different groups, but they can always return to their "home" desk. I tend to make seating assignments in an admittedly undemocratic way at the start of the year by using input from previous teachers to make up the groups. I then tend to leave them alone unless they aren't functional. When that happens, I've sometimes invited the kids to propose new seating arrangements. Remarkably, they often are better than any I could design. These proposal are sensitive to who works well together and who is often left out. More than once I've used these proposals when rearranging the seating. So, while I haven't yet used the technique when creating work groups, I may well do so one day when the moment seems to require it. That moment would depend on the circumstances and the particular personalities of that class of children. A third solution I might well consider with a substantially larger class is to have the kids work in pairs. They can usually manage this better than groups of three and four and with such a challenging project it might be easier to manage with a larger class size.

I don't think I'd plan things differently if I were teaching sections of older children in a departmental setting. Years ago I taught several sections of sixth-grade social studies in just such an environment. Each section did the same projects, and I enjoyed watching how differently each group worked, bringing their own personalities and knowledge to the tasks. For example, studying ancient Rome, each section created a model of a Roman city. I relished helping several sections do this project and seeing the differences from one section to the next.

Q: Would you recommend trying this with a different document, say the Declaration of Independence or one of the problematic treaties made between the U.S. government and American Indians in the nineteenth century?

A: I think it would be fascinating to try this with a different document. Since I work with fourth graders I think one experience like this at the end of the year is enough. My young students use all they've learned about annotating and reading throughout the year to do this project, and it ends up being an informal performance assessment. However, I suspect that older children, with more experience with nonnarrative text, could take this on with more than one document in the course of the year. If I taught our eighth grade U.S. history survey course, for example, I could see creating a number of experiences annotating documents throughout the year, each quite different, but providing students with opportunities to build on previously learned skills.

6

Is That Real?
Literature, History, and Primary Sources

It was very cool to write a book author such as yourself. We got a lot of information about *The Storyteller's Beads*. You were like a human glossary to us. We wish we could meet you in person, but you live so far away. We hope your book is a big success.

Thank you for the shamma and gahbi. It was really fun seeing what those things actually looked like. I think your cover is just great. The pictures look just the way I thought Rahel and Sahay would look. I hope you get nominated for a Newbery award.

We had a lot of fun looking at all the great, interesting things from Ethiopia. We love your finished book. Our favorite objects that you sent were the beads and the spices that smelled great.

Literature, history, and primary sources are a potent mix. Although primary sources are becoming more accepted in upper elementary and middle school social studies programs, they are not similarly considered in literature studies at the same grade levels. Literary scholars rely heavily on primary sources when they dig deeply into particular works of literature, but we don't tend to do the same when studying literature with children. Some of this is due to the legitimate fear that too much analysis can destroy the lived-in literary experience; however, I suspect it is also because those of us who teach literature to children have simply never considered the possibility of using primary sources to do just the opposite: enrich the literary experience.

A lifelong reader, I have always been successful at communicating my enthusiasm and passion for literature to my students. However, I had been teaching for many years before I discovered the potential of primary sources in this curricular area. Just as I increasingly use primary sources in teaching history, I am also using them more and more in literature studies. Some of my methods will no doubt be familiar, since elementary and middle school teachers use primary sources all the time without realizing it. Others may be more surprising, since they are not currently typical classroom practice at these grade levels. However, if we are discovering that elementary and middle school students can learn as much about the past from primary sources as their high school and university counterparts, I have also discovered that something similar is possible in literary studies.

My lack of awareness of primary sources in literature studies was no doubt due to my avoidance of English departments throughout college and graduate school. This unfortunate situation was the sad result of a recommendation from my much admired senior high school English teacher that I not participate in the spring play in order to focus more on my writing. Since I had never been told before that anything was wrong with my writing (other than atrocious spelling), this was quite a shock. And it was compounded because this teacher never explained exactly what was wrong with my writing or helped me to improve it. The result was probably the opposite of what he had intended. Indeed, I did focus more on my writing, but with a remarkable degree of failure: still desperately trying to make an essay better at 2 a.m., I invariably made it worse. My required freshman English class was a nightmare and a special tutorial was recommended; I was told my problem was emotional. Taking the situation into my own hands, I did what most sensible phobics do—avoid its primary cause—and did not take a single English literature course for the rest of my undergraduate and graduate studies.

Fortunately, I took many history courses and through them, became familiar with primary sources, read voraciously on my own, and managed, through various coping mechanisms, to keep my writing phobia under wraps. And in 1990, twenty years after my last encounter with an English literature course, I finally took another: Uli Knoepfmacher's National Endowment for the Humanities (NEH) Seminar at Princeton University, "Classical British and American Children's Literature." I came across the notice unexpectedly and, because of my earlier unsuccessful efforts to become a children' book illustrator, immediately yearned to attend. With the help of two writer friends I managed to write the required essay and ended up spending a magical summer immersed in a new world of scholarship. We met daily in the Firestone Library and grappled with children's literature in a way I had not known was possible, surrounded by literary primary sources. For my final project, I decided to research the illustrators of *Alice's Adventures in Wonderland* and discovered the Rare Book Room. There I spent many happy hours examining illustrated versions of this celebrated text as well as Lewis Carroll's own copy of the published book, full of his tiny writing throughout noting printing errors to be corrected in subsequent printings. Later that summer I traveled to London and visited the British Library to view the original handwritten copy of *Alice's Adventures Underground*.

My NEH Fellowship at Princeton was a watershed. I discovered that I could write an essay acceptable to an English teacher and found a whole new way of looking at books for children. I immediately brought this approach into my classroom and primary sources came along with it. For example, my students and I learn more about *Charlotte's Web* by looking at E. B. White's notes and sketches for the book, letters, photographs of himself and farm, and his many early drafts. Seventeenth- and eighteenth-century versions of *Cinderella* provide us with a fresh look at a familiar story. And outtakes, interviews, and newsreels, take our study comparing Baum's original book and the MGM movie of *The Wizard of Oz* to a very different level. Who would not want to study the original screenplay to figure out why the filmmakers changed the all-important silver shoes in the book to ruby slippers in the movie? (Answer: ruby was more colorful for a Technicolor film.)

A common thread in teaching history and literature is the issue of realness. I want my students to consider the past real, but that becomes more difficult the farther away it is from their own lives. And they want to know about the realness in books. Invariably, the most common questions children's authors get is: Is it real? Primary sources successfully bridge this gap; helping children figure out just what is real.

Literature From and About the Past

Primary sources can enhance the study of any literary genre, but my classroom focus is on those that are from and about the past. *Literature from the past* includes both traditional and classical literature. Today, as we try to provide our students with a more inclusive curriculum, we often disagree about what to do with some of these older works, especially those that are considered great literature but contain sentiments and points of view that are troubling to us today. One solution is to teach them in tandem with other, sometimes less well-known works, that provide alternative perspectives. Another solution is to provide the historical context, so they can be understood as a product of their own times, not ours. Primary sources, I've discovered, can be very effective at providing such context. Children are interested in understanding a work in the context of the time it was written. And by learning the skills of literary criticism they are well armed to deal with such texts if they encounter them on their own.

Literature about the past is a different bird altogether. This is contemporary writing about the past. Historical fiction, biographies, and other sorts of nonfiction fall into this category, but it can get tricky. Works of historical fiction are about the past and reflective of the time in which they were written. The longer ago they were written, the more they may seem like works of the past when they are actually works about the past written in the present. We teachers often use such works with our students with little thought to their accuracy. The best writers of this sort of literature use primary sources in their own research and often include them in the books themselves.

A Sampling of Literary Genres

Traditional Literature

Traditional literature is very popular among elementary teachers. Many of us enjoy bringing folktales, fairy tales, fables, myths, and legends into our classrooms. Not only are they fun and easy to use within a literature program, but such works of traditional literature also enhance history and cultural studies. However one uses such literature in the classroom, the experience can be greatly enriched with primary sources. Primary sources related to traditional literature are plentiful. Students can interview family members to find out what stories they remember from childhood. Facsimiles of older retellings of tales are easy to procure in bookstores, libraries, and even on the Internet. Art is full of images related to traditional literature. It is rich with opportunities for expansion with primary sources.

An example is a unit on Cinderella I've done for many years. I began teaching this unit in 1990. Over the years I have been fortunate enough to receive several NEH fellowships, which enabled me to do research on this ancient tale. While I used to think of it largely in terms of the Perrault version so familiar from the Disney movie, I've since discovered that it is one of the most universal storylines in the world. I've accumulated a vast range of materials to support this unit. In addition to a collection of picture books of Cinderella variants, I have films, facsimiles of seventeenth- and eighteenth-century versions, and many from other countries in languages none of us can read. My students love to pore over these primary sources. They are horrified and intrigued by the Grimm version in which the stepsisters cut off parts of their feet in order to make the glass slipper fit. They are especially intrigued by the difference between a U.S. retelling of a non-Western story and that story as told in its own country. An interesting example is *Yeh-Shen*, a Chinese Cinderella variant. I have two versions of this story, one of which has a page in Chinese at the front. One day, some years ago, I had a visitor from China observing my class as we discussed *Yeh-Shen*. Afterwards she looked at both versions and told me that in the Western versions the story ended long before the Chinese ending with a wedding; whereas in the Chinese original the story went on at length beyond the wedding. Evidently those that retold the story for Western children felt that it should end in a familiar way, not in the real way. Now whenever I use *Yeh-Shen*, I tell my students this story. What may be the *real* Cinderella story to them may be something very different in a different land.

Classical Literature

The definition of "classic" is oft-debated among academics, but for the average teacher it is pretty clear: classics are works that have "stood the test of time." Books that seem to reliably appear on classics lists for middle grade students include Louisa May Alcott's *Little Women*, Francis Burnett's *The Secret Garden*, Jack London's, *The Call of the Wild*, L. Frank Baum's *The Wizard of Oz*, Lewis Carroll's *Alice's Adventures in Wonderland*, and Robert Louis Stevenson's *Kidnapped*. In my school certain teachers require their students to read a set number of books from such a list in the course of the year. I don't have such a requirement for my fourth graders, but I do require them to read every night. Invariably, I have students who read classics purely because they have been told these are very important books to read. In some cases they are sophisticated readers and become truly immersed in the world of *Little Women* or the drama of *Kidnapped*. More frequently, however, I have students plowing through such books with absolutely no sense of what they are about. Or they read abridged and adapted versions of the classics, often altered to such a degree that the authors' voices are lost completely. More often, they know these works through a Disney or some other film adaptation. Demanding that children read such works without providing context could put them off certain authors and even pleasure reading altogether. This concerns me. Many an adult can recollect a negative learning experience with a classic. However, it is possible to set up a stimulating and engaging encounter with many a classic work using primary sources.

A huge fan of *Alice's Adventures In Wonderland*, I have long supplemented my reading aloud of this book with many primary sources. My students are fascinated by the author and the development of the story from something told to three little girls on a picnic one summer day to one of the most well-known children's books of all time. As I read the book aloud, we study different illustrated editions. A favorite is invariably a facsimile of Lewis Carroll's handwritten first version, *Alice's Adventures Underground*. In addition, they enjoy seeing photographs of Carroll and of Alice Liddell, the real Alice, and her sisters. In 1998 I spent a week at Christ Church, Oxford, where Lewis Carroll, whose real name was Charles L. Dodgson, lived and wrote. While there, I discovered that many incidents and places in *Alice* related to various places and things in Oxford. My students love hearing about my firsthand experience of these places as I read the book to them. Over the years I've gotten to know librarians at various research institutions and often take my students to their rare book rooms to see some of their Lewis Carroll holdings. My students are thrilled to see the real first editions of *Alice* and other materials associated with the book and its author.

Lewis Carroll was a prolific letter writer, especially to children. Upon concluding the most recent reading of *Alice's Adventures in Wonderland*, I suggested that the students write letters to Lewis Carroll or Alice Liddell. First I showed them several copies of letters Carroll had written to children from Christina Bjork's *The Other Alice: The Story of Alice Liddell and Alice in Wonderland*. He was a remarkably clever letter writer. Not only do his letters have wonderful stories and humor on a par with the most clever parts of the *Alice* books, but they are often visually clever as well. He wrote children backward letters, rebus letters, and circular letters. I then read to them part of a small pamphlet Lewis Carroll wrote to accompany a commercial product that promoted his book, The Wonderland Postage Stamp Case. There are two parts to the case, an outside and an interior pocket. The exterior has Tenniel's Cheshire Cat on it, while the an interior packet has the disappearing Cat. By pulling out the interior pocket you can simulate the Cat's disappearing act. The children adored seeing photographs of this. The pamphlet written to accompany this clever product is titled *Eight or Nine Wise Words about Letter -Writing*. It provides many sensible suggestions that are still useful today such as: "When you take your letters to the Post, carry them in your hand. If you put them in your pocket you will take a long country walk, passing the Post-Office twice, going and returning, and, when you return home, will still find them in your pocket." One that especially intrigued my students was the admonishment "don't cross. Remember the old proverb, 'Cross-writing makes cross reading.' 'The old proverb?' you say, inquiringly. 'How old?' Well, not so very ancient, I must confess. In fact, I'm afraid I invented it while writing this paragraph!" Returning to the facsimiles of the letters we discovered an example of cross writing: having reached the end of the page, rather than continuing on another sheet, one turns the page sideways writing perpendicularly through the previous writing.

The children, after hearing all of this, wrote their own letters to one of the two most important people associated with *Alice*, Lewis Carroll and Alice Liddell. Several wrote their final copies in purple ink to honor Carroll, who wrote in purple ink from 1871 to 1891. One or two pleaded to be allowed to cross-write, but I was firm: Carroll disapproved and so did I. However, Nicolai was sufficiently inspired to imitate Carroll's language and his visually unusual letters. Nicolai's original letter appears in Figure 6-1 (with my transcription below in which I have corrected his mechanical errors so that it is easier to read). He has done a remarkably clever job of imitating Carroll's Victorian style, complete with abbreviations.

Dear Alice Liddell,

Hello. My name is Nicolai. I loved that book your dear friend, Lewis Carroll made. It was absolutely wonderful.

It was also funny.

How did you feel when L.C. wrote about you? What of your friends? If they thought it was dry . . . DITTO!

I think A.W. I. [was] great because of the H. [Hatter], the C [Cheshire Cat], and Alice.

Sincerely N. S.

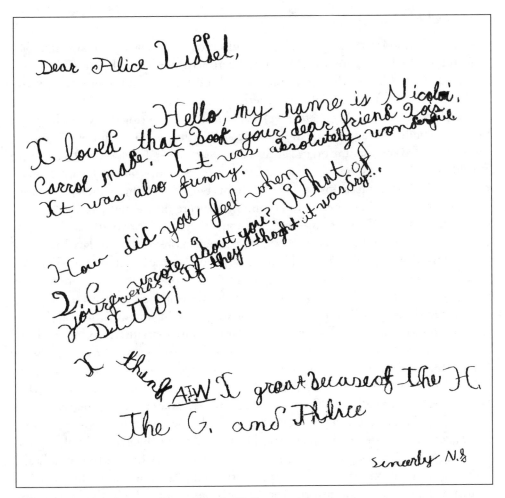

Figure 6–1. Nicolai's Letter to Alice Liddell

I do offer, though, a warning about the use of classical literature. These works reflect the attitudes of their authors in the times they were written. In some cases, books despite recognized works of art are shied away from because of this. Mark Twain's *Huckleberry Finn*, for example, is often challenged because of its derogatory language. However, careful use of primary sources can provide the crucial historical context students need to understand exactly why Twain used such language. Age appropriateness needs to be considered as well. I would certainly not use *Huckleberry Finn* with nine year olds, whereas I well might with sixteen year olds, developmentally far better prepared to understand the complexities of language and racism in our past and in our literature.

Historical Fiction

Historical fiction is a tricky genre. Such works provide a view into a past time, but reflected through the time in which they were written. Thus, Karen Cushman's *Catherine, Called Birdy* offers young readers a well-researched presentation of the Middle Ages and a feisty, late-twentieth-century-style heroine. The historian James Lincoln Collier's *My Brother Sam Is Dead*, written during the Vietnam War, provides a multifaceted view of the American Revolution quite different from the more one-sided representation in Esther Forbes' in *Johnny Tremain*, written during World War II. Gail Carson Levine, in *Dave at Night*, writes about Jewish Americans and African Americans in 1926 Harlem, but at any time many years later, when relations between these two communities were occasionally tense. In a recent conversation, Gail told me that relations between the two ethnic groups at the time her novel takes place were close, perhaps more so than today. In "Writing Backward: Modern Models in Historical Fiction" Anne Scott MacLeod (1998) cogently reviews this problem and reminds us that "people of the past were not just us in odd clothing. They were people who saw the world differently; approached human relationships differently; people for whom night and day, heat and cold, seasons and work and play had meanings lost to an industrialized world" (p. 33).

On occasion I have used historical fiction that strikes an achronistic chord. When this happens I usually point it out to my students and ask them what they think. For example, we read Kathryn Lasky's (1996), *Journey to the New World: The Diary of Remember Patience Whipple* after my students have been immersed in the world of the Plimoth settlers of 1620. Having had a great deal of exposure to first-hand accounts, they easily wonder whether it would have been very likely for Patience to make her own way to an Indian settlement or whether that was Lasky providing a situation for late twentieth-century female readers more in need of a historical role model than historical accuracy. I have found that providing a classroom environment where authors are considered real people who can be challenged and students have ample primary source material makes historical fiction an intriguing part of a history program.

I tend to favor using historical fiction only after children have already become experts through immersion in a particular era. Then historical fiction can provide another view and wonderful models for children attempting to write original works of historical fiction themselves. I seem to have a minority viewpoint, however. Many teachers and teacher educators are very much in favor of using historical fiction as a motivating device to introduce a unit . Their feeling seems to be that only a fictionalized account will engage childrens' imaginations about the past. While I would agree that story and narration is a fine way to begin a unit, I disagree strongly that it must be fiction. In my opinion there are any number of wonderful firsthand accounts that can engage childrens' imaginations. Some of those who argue so strongly in favor of using historical fiction to launch historical studies do so, I suspect, because of their own deeply rooted views that history is inherently boring and dull (most likely the result of bad and truly boring textbook-based school history courses) and that only fiction can spice it up. To me history is exciting, fascinating, and stimulating all by itself and needs no fictionalizing whatsoever.

I'm also skittish about beginning a history unit with historical fiction because I want my students to construct their own versions of the past. Providing them with a prepackaged view absolves them from creating one of their own. The historical fiction author hands them the ideas on a platter. This, I hasten to add, has nothing to do with the authors and everything to do with us, the teachers. Some historical fiction authors write primarily to instruct, but the best write because some past event has inspired them to create a work of art. These artists, while certainly interested in how their works are used by teachers, are not teachers themselves. As teachers, we can use these works to promote a particular point of view, to model a kind of history writing, or to dig deep into history. I would argue for immersing children in a particular era and giving plenty of primary sources. Only then, after they have had time to construct their own view, would I bring in historical fiction. This is what I did with Kathryn Lasky's *Journey to a New World*. My students also did research projects on the Wampanoags before I read aloud Michael Dorris's *Guests*, a work of historical fiction providing the Native American view of the harvest feast on which the Thanksgiving holiday is based.

Fictional Memoirs and Fictional Family History

Fictionalized memoirs are especially effective means of deepening students' understanding of the past. As students work on their own immigrant oral histories, they enjoy reading fiction based on the author's own immigration experience or that of someone in his or her family. Karen Hesse's *Letters from Rifka*, Kathryn Lasky's *The Night Journey*, and Bette Bao Lord's *In the Year of the Boar and Jackie Robinson* all work for my students because of the personal history that underlies the fictional story. Visits to Ellis Island, the Lower East Side Tenement Museum, and a video about Angel Island in San Francisco further ground these stories and connect them to the ones my students are discovering through their own oral history interviews.

An especially popular fiction series based on memory is Laura Ingalls Wilder's *Little House* books. But Wilder wrote her books many years after the events on which they are based took place. This means that her point of view, toward Native Americans for example, reflects her own at the time of writing, a harsh one not untypical of settlers. However, these descriptions are quite troubling to Native Americans today, some of whom have argued for their removal from school curricula. Although I have not used these books with my students, I have paid close attention to these Native American voices, and I am convinced that teachers using these books must be sure to place them in historical context and provide alternative points of view. There are plenty of instructional materials, including primary sources, available. The 1892 Homestead Act might be a good place to start followed by a discussion about what *home* means and different perspectives on land ownership. Another possibility might be to contrast the *Little House* books with Louise Erdrich's recent *The Birchbark House* , based on her own Native American heritage, along with the memoir "Impressions of an Indian Childhood," an *Atlantic Monthly* article from 1900 by Zitkala-Sa.

Biography and Other Nonfiction Historical Narratives

At Her Majesty's Request: An African Princess in Victorian England by Walter Dean Myers is a fine, well-researched example of a biography for children that incorporates primary sources in a rich and compelling way. Sarah Forbes Bonetta, Myers discovers, was from West Africa. A British naval officer happened upon her as she was about to be killed in a ritual and in response to his concern, the girl is presented to him as a gift for his queen, Victoria. Myers first became aware of Sarah when he was told of a series of letters about her that were available for purchase. In the introduction, he tells of his efforts to learn more about this woman's extraordinary life after buying her letters. An English researcher he hired knew about the girl's school, the Royal Archives at Windsor Castle had photographs of Sarah and her daughter, and she was mentioned in Queen Victoria's diary. Through diligent and methodical research, Myers pieced together the facts. The resulting book is a true story that draws on many primary sources.

Another fine example of nonfiction utilizing primary sources is *Breaking Ground, Breaking Silence: The Story of New York's African Burial Ground* by Joyce Hansen and Gary McGowan. The African Burial Ground was discovered in 1991 during excavation for a new building. Eighteenth-century city maps had indicated a "Negro Burying Ground," but the original archaeologists did not expect to find much more than a handful of graves. They were wrong: more than four hundred graves were eventually excavated. The resulting publicity stopped both the excavation and the construction to allow time for a thoughtful decision on what to do. Finally, construction plans were reworked and the building finished in 1994, included a memorial honoring those buried. The excavated remains went to Howard University, where they have been studied by archaeologists, anthropologists, and historians. This book provides the story of the excavation itself, the stories of those who were buried at the site, and the larger story, too often untold, of Africans in colonial times. The authors note that the information gleaned from the burial ground has provided a way to redress the written record: "In a sense, it is as though the people who have been written out of history have found a way to tell us about themselves through the objects buried with them" (p. 10). This book, carefully and thoughtfully researched and written, gives students a unique way to learn about the African colonial experience. It includes many photographs of the burials, eighteenth-century maps, art, and written documents.

Myra Zarnowski, a professor at Queens College in New York City, is a strong advocate of using good nonfiction historical narratives in elementary and middle school classrooms, but she also argues strongly that both children and their teachers should be alert to possible historical inaccuracies in the books they read. In "Coming Out From Under the Spell of Stories: Critiquing Historical Narratives" Zarnowski makes a compelling case for creating a classroom environment in which students are encouraged to develop critical skills when reading history. She recommends that teachers point out the source notes in the books children read and even read some of the primary sources cited. This will help children to understand the process of writing history: "copying from an encyclopedia or any single source, or even paraphrasing one by changing a word here or there—a common and durable practice—is not what is meant by writing history. Instead, a writer must be both a sifter and a shaper of information" (p. 348). And certainly, sifting through primary sources and then shaping the resulting narrative is what good writers of history for children do. Good biographies and other nonfiction history books can provide children with wonderful examples of what it is to write history.

The Storyteller's Beads

The big brown box arrived in our classroom at the end of April, and the students were beside themselves with excitement. They knew what was inside: Ethiopian artifacts from Jane Kurtz, the "real stuff" she so wonderfully described in *The Storyteller's Beads*. I'd just finished reading aloud the prepublication galleys, which swept us off to Ethiopia in the 1980s, during a terrible time of drought and war. My students had corresponded with Jane about the details of the book, her creative development, her research, and her childhood in Ethiopia. It had been an extraordinary experience for them. Suddenly this story, set in a far removed time and place, began to seem less like a fairy tale and more like something real. Yet, we still didn't quite have it all in place. As vivid as Jane's descriptions were, my students hungered for more. And some of those missing pieces, we had no doubt, were in that box. With great care we opened it. There, on top nestled among the soft cotton shamma cloth, was a shiny new book, one of the very first copies of *The*

Storyteller's Beads, inscribed, "To Monica and her students, who—except for editors and a few friends—gave me my precious first reader feedback! May your stories keep you strong! Jane Kurtz."

For every rule there is an exception, especially in teaching. After writing passionately a few pages back about my aversion to using historical fiction to initiate a study, I did just that with *The Storyteller's Beads.* And given a similar opportunity, I'd break my rule yet again without a moment's hesitation. Teachers operate according to many personal rules. Along with providing a predictable, orderly, and understandable learning environment, we also need to be flexible, not only for the crying child, the distressed parent, the special event, but for the unique opportunity. Yes, I still feel that historical fiction should be used judiciously, well into a unit, but I also believe in *carpe diem,* that we teachers must grab the teachable moment. Such was the situation with Jane Kurtz's *The Storyteller's Beads.*

In March 1998, I had received a private e-mail from Jane, someone I knew solely through the on-line Internet discussion group, Child_lit. Subscribers since 1994, we had both been active participants in many strident, contentious, yet interesting conversations. Currently a resident of North Dakota, Jane grew up in a remote part of Ethiopia, the daughter of missionaries, and she is the author of several books set in Ethiopia. When disagreements erupted on Child_lit over how to present different cultures to American children, especially those far away, Jane and I had often agreed. Most likely, our mutual experiences of living as outsiders in Africa connected us as well.

Jane's e-mail to me was an invitation to read a prepublication copy of her new middle grade book, *The Storyteller's Beads,* to my class. She was interested in getting a group of children to respond to this, her first book for older readers. I responded cautiously, not quite sure how the book's topic and setting would fit into my students' studies. We had just completed our intensive study of the Pilgrims, and my students were still beaming with pride over their carefully researched works of historical fiction that drew on primary sources. They knew about historical fiction, how to critique it as well as how to write it themselves. Jane's invitation arrived just as we were about to move on to our final units of the year. I had planned to follow a study of the Constitution with a look at the Civil Rights Movement as a social studies unit and in language arts to look at memoir. Both studies were intended to continued our yearlong musings about the nature of history. In the case of the Constitution (see Chapter 5), my students would be grappling with the document and its place in our national history while memoirs would provide another look at personal history.

Interested, but somewhat dubious as to how this could quite connect to Jane's book, I wrote her describing my plans. Here are some excerpts from her response:

I don't know how much you get into the whole issue of prejudice when you talk about Civil Rights, but I think of BEADS as very much a book about prejudice. In fact, one thing that intrigued me and set the idea spinning in my mind was when I read in an ethnography about the Kaman that the Kaman say the Beta-Israel are possessed of an evil eye, while the Amhara say the Kemant (as well as the Beta-Israel) are possessed of an evil eye. It fascinated me to think. . . . what if there were a girl who grew up in the very protected Kemant community, secure in her prejudice, who in being thrown into the wider world discovered, to her shock, that other people saw her in exactly the same way? I think we often tend to present prejudice as a western thing or as a white against people of color thing. To me, it's clearly a human condition thing. . . .

The memoir thing is strong, too . . . the idea that we must tell our stories and we must hang onto our personal stories and those of our heritage. I read countless accounts of survivors, and the other thing that made me obsessed with writing this book was one sentence about a blind girl who walked all the way to Sudan with her hand on her brother's shoulder. I find kids are fascinated with the line between fiction and nonfiction and love to see how I have put real people into my books or how, for instance, the illustrator for TROUBLE took a real woman from a photograph and put her into the wedding scene. When I was out in California, a teacher told me that ONLY A PIGEON had been her students' favorite of my books, and when I asked if she had any idea why, she said, "I think it's the photo of the real boy at the back of the book. They always are intrigued by that question of 'what's real?'". . . .

The other connection, of course, is that the 1980s in Ethiopia are a part of my personal history that I've been reluctant to write about, a story I've been reluctant to tell. Since the only thing people here tend to know about Ethiopia is "starving children," I've wanted to show that there's much more to Ethiopia. But this book can also be seen as finally my attempt to bring that part of my own history to life, to make it more real for other people.

Please know I'll be happy to help—I can loan you things from Ethiopia, if you have time to do something like that. They can look at a shamma and a gahbi, at the black clay pots, at amber beads, at photos. This kind of thing is terrific fun for me.

With that I was hooked. My rule not to use historical fiction before knowing something about the time and the place went out the window. What an opportunity, I thought, to watch and interact with a writer who uses her personal past as well as careful research with primary sources about a part of the world neither my students nor I, for that matter, knew much about. We had been taking about history all year, with a special emphasis on sources. Here was a chance to learn about a historical event for which there were firsthand accounts not unlike those my students had come across in our other studies during the year. I also felt that my students, many of whom were Jewish, would have a particular interest in learning about Rahel's people, the Beta-Israel, Ethiopian Jews. With no time to prepare, I simply dived in. Jane sent the book and a week or so after her initial invitation I had begun reading it aloud to the class.

The galleys came without the map and the glossary that would be part of the final book. My students became fascinated about exactly where the story took place and sought out maps in our school library and on the Internet to find the real places described in the story. The unfamiliar Amharic (the official language of Ethiopia) words that Jane sprinkled throughout the text also intrigued them. I began a glossary chart and added to it as we made our way through the book. The children wanted to know more about Jane, so in addition to the answers she provided in her letters, we turned to her Web site, which gave us photographs and more of her personal history. I also found several of her other books in our school library. *Only Pigeon*, a picture book, was a sensitive retelling of an Ethiopian folktale, which Jane recalled from her childhood in Ethiopia. We also discovered her informational book *Ethiopia: Roof of Africa*. Yet these sources paled in comparison with Jane herself. At three points during my reading of the story, the children wrote to her. Each time, she wrote back a brief personal note to each child, full of information in response to their many questions. She sent drafts of the first chapter so the children could see how the story evolved, and then wrote more about this creative process in her letters. The culminating piece was the box of artifacts. By then, Jane had become close to us in many ways.

The Storyteller's Beads is the story of Sahay and Rahel, two girls from different ethnic groups who are forced to depend on each other when making a long and arduous trek to a refugee camp in Sudan. Rahel, blind most of her life, is an Ethiopian Jew, while Sahay is Kemant, another marginalized cultural group. Both are very suspicious of one another initially, but become friends during their long ordeal. Jane researched firsthand refugee accounts in creating the story and called upon her own childhood memories of Ethiopia. The book begins with Sahay's story, continues with Rahel's, and then becomes both of their stories. It is an interesting construct, as the girls are dual protagonists, but neither dominates the other. Although the story is written in the third person, my students were so captivated by it and felt so much a part of it and so lived in the story that some seemed to think it was first person: first Sahay's voice, then Rahel's, then both girls.

The Storyteller's Beads Chart

Our glossary chart filled up with words and phrases that interested us, that helped us organize the story path, and some we weren't so sure about and hoped to learn more from Jane and from further research.

Sahay's Story	Rahel's Story
Parents and brother killed.	Parents and grandparents stay behind.
Flees with uncle, but he turns back.	Flees with brother, who is forced back
Nahase (12th month)	Falasha (Ethiopian Jew)
food: arah, saweh	food: injera, wat
markato (market)	kes (cantor?)
shiftas (thieves)	aliyah (go to Israel)
gahbi, shamma (cloaks)	baaltet (wise older woman)
tukul (house)	Beta-Israel
Addis Ababa	Fasika festival (Passover?)
Red Terror	
buda (person with the evil eye)	

Other words that interested us or about which we wanted to know more:

famine	drought	White Terror	Ayezoch	shammas
Red Cross	Sudan	Eritrea	Atbara River	
Ethiopia	Umm Rekuba (mother of shelter)			

plants	*animals*	*illness*
eucalyptus trees	lions	river blindness?
acacia	hyenas	bilharzia (schistosomiasis)
	snakes	malaria

Our Correspondence with Jane

The children wrote letters to Jane three times: at two points during the reading of the book and a final response at the end. Their letters were handwritten and I sent them via regular mail. Jane responded through e-mail and, in one case when she was traveling, in a handwritten letter. These letters were always to the whole class with references by name to each child and his or her letter, so that she did not answer questions more than once. Jane's letters were primary sources for us. They provided us with firsthand information about Ethiopia, and about her writing process.

First Set of Letters The children wrote the first letters after they had heard the first third of the book, the separate stories of the two girls. Jane had sent us three different drafts of the first chapter, Sahay's story, which we enjoyed comparing to what I had been reading aloud. My students were fascinated by the differences, most of all the change in voice from first person to third. The children were completing their own works of historical fiction based on our study of the Pilgrims, in addition to enjoyment so they were very interested in her writing process as it related to their own.

April 16, 1998

Dear Jane,

My name is Mara. Our class is studying the Pilgrims. Even though you are writing a sort of memoir and we are writing time travel stories [about the Pilgrims] they are similar because they involve composite characters and tell about a true time.

I love your dramatic first chapter. I love how it makes you want to read on.

Why did you switch from first person to third? Is the Fasika festival Passover? Is a "kes" a cantor? What is the Red Terror? What is the White Terror?

Thank you,
Mara

April 16, 1998

Dear Jane,

Hello! My name is Emily and I've learned a lot about Ethiopia by reading some of your book. It was not a subject I particularly would have chosen to read about, but now that my teacher has read a little bit of it I would love to learn more about Africa.

Certain parts of *The Storyteller's Beads* remind me of the book *Guests* [by Michael Dorris]. Rahel and her grandmother remind me of the story [in *Guests*] about how there came to be the different clans. The title (which I don't know why it was named that yet) reminds me of when Moss breaks the storybeads.

I have a few questions which I hope you don't mind answering. Does falasha mean Jew or just strange or alien? Why did you switch from first person to third person in different drafts of the first chapter? What does the clothing and architecture of Ethiopia look like?

Thank you for reading my letter.

Yours,
Emily

April 16, 1998

Dear Ms. Kurtz,

My name is Daniel and I go to the Dalton School. I like history (partly European history) and I like to read.

I like your book and the sense of mystery in it. I think that Ethiopia reminds me of Nazi Germany because Jewish schools are being closed. There's an anti-Semitic feeling among Christians and Jews are trying to get out of the country.

Is Falasha a term only referring to Jews or just anybody alien? What was your first book called? When you were in Ethiopia did you experience any long droughts or famines?

I think that your book is really good and has wonderful description.

Yours,
Daniel

April 21 and 23, 1998

Dear Students in Monica's Class. . . .

I LOVED reading your letters. It is so fun, for an author, to know what people are thinking as they read. While we work, we usually work all alone in a room with only words, so it's a big mystery, in some ways, what people are going to think when they read the words. . . .

Mara (and others) the switch from first to third happened because at first I only wrote Sahay's story and everything was in her point of view. But then my editor wanted me to write Rahel's point of view too. So it seemed easier to write in third person, then. A "kes" is like a rabbi. . . .

Emily, the clothing of Ethiopians is mostly white (cotton) with colorful borders. If you get a chance to see my picture books, you can see examples of what it looks like. . . .

Daniel, my very first book of all was called *Trinidad: Stories of the Past.* It had a soft cover and was about the town in Colorado where I was living.

Several people asked questions that were about how the first chapter changed so I thought I'd explain a little of how the book turned into the novel it became. I wrote the first draft only from Sahay's point of view. At the same time I wrote a short story about a girl who had to flee from Ethiopia and her grandmother told her a story and gave her beads to give her courage. The short story turned into a chapter book. My editor read the chapter book right after she had agreed to publish my novel and she wanted me to try making the novel and the chapter book one book! So I thought I was writing two books and I ended up with one book from two points of view. Maybe it sounds easy. It wasn't! I did at least four major revisions to make it all work. . . .

The main reason the girls have so much in common is that kids in Ethiopia from different ethnic groups *do* have lives that are very similar. . . . but they don't realize that. I wanted to show that Rahel is a lot like Sahay—but Sahay doesn't know that. Sahay has been raised to think Rahel's people are scary and have mysterious powers and will do evil things. As Daniel said, that kind of fear and prejudice reminds us of Nazi Germany and maybe of people here in the U.S. that other people think must be scary or bad just because of their different traditions and background, right?

Yours,
Jane

Second Set of Letters The children wrote their second set of letters to Jane after I had read Part III, where the two girls meet and reluctantly join forces. In preparation, the children and I reviewed the book thus far, and I took the following notes of our conversation on chart paper:

> *Things to keep in mind when writing second letter to Jane. (Be sure to comment on the book; don't just ask questions.)*
> Review of book so far:
> Parts I and II were separate on Sahay and Rahel.
> Part III alternated chapters about each girl. First meeting was from Sahay's point of view.
> Questions that came up during the reading:
> What about Rahel's blindness? Did Jane have a particular illness in mind? Did Jane know of situations like this?
> Are Sahay and Rahel composite characters of real people that were interviewed?
> Connection to Holocaust.
> Wondered about hyenas.
> Wondered if Jane had been in the areas where the story took place. Or if she had simply done research on the areas.

April 24, 1998

Dear Jane,

Hi again. Thank you for responding to our letters. Though I did not get much of one I did enjoy listening to the others. This time Ms. Edinger promises to put my letter on the top of the pile.

I am liking the book more and more as we go on. I am really feeling there. We just read a little about the soldiers taking the men away. And I am wondering how I would feel if someone from my family or someone I knew was being taken away and I would never see them ever again.

Here are some more questions. Are the characters in *The Storyteller's Beads* composite? Did you ever have an experience with hyenas since you write a lot about them?

Thanks a lot again,

Becky

April 24, 1998

Dear Ms. Kurtz,

Thank you for taking the time to write back. I know my teacher and I really appreciate it also.

Here are some questions about the book. The river that they crossed, is it a real river and if it is what is it called? Did your editor decide Rahel was going to be blind or did you? By the way, what disease made her blind, if any one did? Have you ever had an experience with hyenas?

I love your book. It is really touching. I think it helps people understand the awful things that happen to people around the world. You have the coolest vocabulary ever.

> Thank you again.
> Sincerely,
> William

April 24, 1998

Dear Jane,

It's Keith again. I would like to thank you for responding to my letter. Some times if you write to an author or a sports player it takes so long for them to write you back. Sometimes you never get a letter back.

The book keeps getting better and better. First it started out slow. I don't mean boring slow, I mean slow slow. Then it went right into action and went quickly. It never went by too fast.

When the editor wants to change something you really like to do you get upset?

> Keith

April 29, 1998

Hello, everyone.

I hope you got my letter that I sat in my B&B room in Kansas and wrote to all of you. I got your second pack of letters yesterday, and today shouldn't be quite as rushed in answering. Thanks for your patience when my replies are short. I sent one of the very first copies of the novel off to you yesterday, along with some things I'm loaning you so you can experience Ethiopia a bit more. . . .

Becky, your letter was right on top, just like you said! Yes, I wondered too, how I would feel if someone from my family was being taken away. . . . I think part of Rahel and Sahay must hang onto the hope that it isn't forever, don't you? I did have to go to boarding school from 4th grade on (in Addis Ababa) and only see my parents twice a year, so I drew on those feelings when I wrote that scene. And, yes, I'd say all the characters pick up pieces of real people I've met or read about — myself, my sisters, my friends, and those who survived the journey. Hyenas were a big part of my life in Ethiopia. I heard them almost every night as I was going to sleep in Addis Ababa. When I got to speak in Ethiopia last year, I asked the librarian in the International School if she could help me get a tape of hyena calls because I'd like to be able to share that strange sound. Have any of you heard it?

William, yes the Atbara River is real. In some years, it was a raging river that people had to struggle to cross. But, as you know, in the year that Rahel and Sahay escaped, it was all dried up. In my author note, you'll see where I got that idea. I talked earlier in this letter about what made her blind and about the hyenas. I think "touching" is a really good word to use to describe the book. My editor said she cried even when she read the last version, which was about the 5th time she had to read the book. I cried more than once when I was working on it. It's a sad story, isn't it? Thanks for the comment on the "coolest vocabulary."

Keith, I know what you mean about this quick response. Isn't e-mail great? People are so busy that many times you DON'T hear back quickly, or even at all. I'm glad to hear that you think the book is getting better and better. Yes, I do get upset sometimes when my editor suggests a change. Sometimes I immediately think, "yes!" It makes me see my own story in a new way. But sometimes I don't want to make the change or I can't see how to make the change. Sometimes I get up and storm around my office because it's tooooooooooo hard. Do you ever feel that way? I didn't really use another plot or story, but I did remember something another author once said at a conference: never forget what your main character longs for and wants more than anything.

Jane

The Final Response We had just finished the book when Jane's box of artifacts arrived. The children simply loved sifting through them, feeling the soft cloth, touching the smooth amber beads, examining the clay pot, smelling the spices, and studying the photographs. We then tried to decide just what we could do to thank Jane and communicate our feelings about her book and our whole experience with her. Finally the children decided that each would make a bead out of construction paper, write a note to Jane on the inside and decorate the outside. They invested much energy and care in each bead. They wrote poems, quotes from the books with illustrations, and final letters to Jane on the insides and colored the outsides in full. We rolled each one into a bead and strung them on a large piece of string. We sent this final response to Jane with the following heartfelt instructions from the class: "Here are *our* storyteller's beads. Untie each and there will be a letter, poem and/or picture inside. We hope you enjoy them."

The Blue Nile

Our continuing conversations about Jane Kurtz, her book, and Ethiopia caused me to ask my students if they would be interested in going to an Ethiopian restaurant. They were most enthusiastic. I warned them that the food would be very different from what they were used to. It would be spicy and involve eating with their hands. With their enthusiasm undiminished I arranged a lunch at The Blue Nile, a local

Figure 6–2. The Inside of Mara's Bead

"My grandmother fell beside one cousin, with her arms around my youngest cousin. The strangers had killed them all...."

Your book portrayed something I had only seen on the news.

I could feel Sahay and Rahel so well. I might as well have been there, holding Rahel's hand, just like Sahay. The pain and the scar was so real.

Figure 6–3. The Inside of Emily's Bead

Ethiopian restaurant. The proprietors were very kind, opening the establishment specially for us. The children arrived and were immediately charmed by the low stools and basket tables around which they sat ready to eat in the communal fashion of Ethiopia. Soon came large platters of injera, the special spongy bread of Ethiopian cuisine, which they used to scoop up and eat traditional dishes made of red lentils, lamb and chicken, and peas, seasoned with many of the very same spices Jane had sent in her box. Now the foods mentioned in her book were on their very tongues. It was a wonderful and most appropriate (primary source) ending for our literary adventure with Jane Kurtz and *The Storyteller's Beads*.

Reflections on Realness

The Ethiopia of Jane's book became real to my students. The texture and taste of injera, the smooth touch of amber beads, the smell of spices, the look of a shamma, and the details of photographs moved them beyond a good story well told to the place behind the story. Ethiopia, I suspect and hope, will now always be a bit more familiar, not another far off and alien place occasionally on the news. And the work of a writer became real too. Jane's generosity with her early drafts and thoughtful responses to the children's letters helped them to see more closely the real work that goes on behind the books they read.

Will's final response, which he put inside his storyteller bead, movingly expresses what all of us felt by the end of the unit.

> **Story Teller's Beads**
> Touching
> Or happy
> Rahel
> Yeah for Ms. Kurtz!
> Totally inspiring!
> Everybody
> Loved it
> Like I'm living the story
> Exciting
> Realistically fantastic
> Sahay
> Best story I've ever heard
> Emotional
> A truly great book
> Dumbfounding
> So mysterious

Questions & Answers

Q: I'm not anywhere near any archives, research libraries, or universities. How do you suggest I begin finding literary primary sources to use with my students as you did?

A: The best place to start is the Internet. Every day another archive gets a collection on-line. And even if you can't find the primary source you want on-line, you will very likely find out where it is. It may well take a bit of time and good search strategies, but the material is out there. Many superb children's literature sites exist, some of which are accessible through this book's accompanying CD. Literary societies, such as the Lewis Carroll Society of North America, maintain sites in where many of resources are available.

Another way to discover literary primary sources is simply to let people around you know of your interests. My collection of illustrated copies of *Alice's Adventure's in Wonderland* is frequently enlarged by someone who has heard of my interest and gives me an old copy he or she knows I would appreciate. Or a family member will bring a particularly treasured edition to school to show the class. I also suggest scouring yard sales, flea markets, and the like. My collection is full of books I've discovered in such obscure places.

Q: How do you suggest connecting to real authors as you did with Jane Kurtz?

A: Funny you should ask! Jane has co-authored a book with librarian Toni Buzzeo called *Terrific Connections with Authors, Illustrators, and Storytellers: Real Space and Virtual Links* (1999) which is full of great ideas on making these sorts of author connections. You can even read about *The Storyteller's Beads* project from Jane's perspective. "Though famous authors juggle many demands on their time—too many to accommodate all of them—authors or illustrators who are just beginning their careers are often eager to connect with their readers" (p. xi). The book is sprinkled with quotes from interviews Toni and Jane did with educators and bookpeople. There are chapters on author visits, how to select the right bookperson, curriculum connections, e-mail and snail mail opportunities and Web sites. It is an outstanding resource for teachers interested in making the sort of author-class connection we made with Jane.

Q: You and Jane met on Child_lit. Can you tell me more about this group?

A: Child_lit is described by its creator Michael Joseph, a rare book librarian at Rutger's University, as "an unmoderated discussion group convened for the express purpose of examining the theory and criticism of literature for children and young adults." It functions as a mailing list, which means participants communicate by e-mail. It is emphatically not the place to gain information available from libraries or other sources. Rather, it is a place to converse about interesting and complex issues revolving around children's literature. Jane and I got to know each other because we had both participated in threads related to multiculturalism and historical fiction. The best way to learn more about Child_lit is to visit the Child_lit Web site <www.rci.rutgers.edu/~mjoseph/childlit/about.html> and explore the archives. They give a good sense of the sort of discourse involved. If, after that, you wish to subscribe, the information on how to do so is also on the Web site.

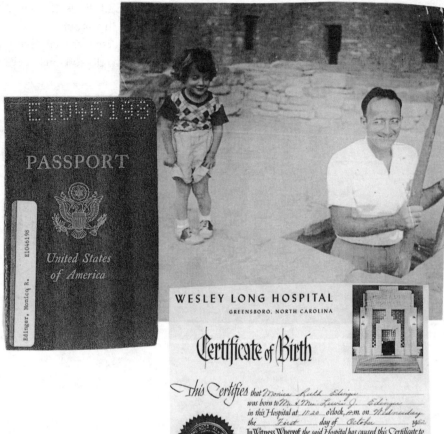

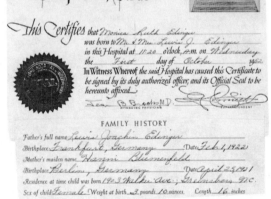

WESLEY LONG HOSPITAL
GREENSBORO, NORTH CAROLINA

Certificate of Birth

This Certifies that *Monica Ruth Edinger*
was born to *Mr. & Mrs. Lewis J. Edinger*
in this Hospital at *11:20* o'clock, *a.m.* on *Wednesday*
the *First* day of *October* *1952*
In Witness Whereof the said Hospital has caused this Certificate to
be signed by its duly authorized officer, and its Official Seal to be
hereunto affixed.

Jean B. Brown M.D.
ATTENDING PHYSICIAN

J. Wright
SUPERINTENDENT

FAMILY HISTORY

Father's full name *Lewis Joachim Edinger*
Birthplace *Frankfurt, Germany* Date *Feb 1, 1922*
Mother's maiden name *Hanni Blumenfeld*
Birthplace *Berlin, Germany* Date *April 25, 1921*
Residence at time child was born *1903 Walker Ave.; Greensboro N.C.*
Sex of child *Female* Weight at birth *3* pounds *10* ounces Length *16* inches

Afterword

Another passport. United States of America is printed on its green cover and there is another eagle as well, an American eagle with *E Pluribis Unum* on a ribbon floating behind. When I open it up, the first thing that catches my eye is my picture and the date it was issued: May 14, 1974. It is my Peace Corps passport, full of employment permits for Sierra Leone, visas, and entry and exit stamps for Gambia, Senegal, Mali, and other countries I visited at that time. Memories flood back unchecked as I leaf through it.

A photograph. Of my father and a very young me at Mesa Verde. I study the photograph and notice how much my father looks like his father in the photographs I have of him. I wonder. Were their personalities also so similar?

My birth certificate. Monica Ruth Edinger, born on October 1, 1952, in Greensboro, North Carolina. Mother born in Berlin, Germany. Father born in Frankfurt, Germany. We move on. While my grandfather may have perished in the Holocaust, his son did not. Instead, he came to America. There he met my mother and together they produced me: first generation American.

My Peace Corps passport, the photo at Mesa Verde, and my birth certificate are a collage of my personal history: one of optimism despite a disturbing family events. Out of the depths of the Holocaust my German family has been remade American. While the collage of father's Nazi passport, my grandfather's photo, and his letter evoke feelings of sadness, this collage of Peace Corps, family, and birth evokes feelings of happiness. Primary sources enable me to turn despair into hope, sorrow into joy.

The past is alive and well in our culture. It turns up in movies, in books, on the Internet, and in our everyday lives. Sometimes it is as personal as a passport, while at other times it is as remote as the images on television of armed conflicts in far away places. It can be as local as the revitalization of Main Street or as far away as the truth about the relationship between Sally Hemmings and Thomas Jefferson. It comes up in thoughtful ways and in not-so-thoughtful ways. As a teacher, my hope is to help my students to be thoughtful about the history they see represented around them: to wonder about it, to inquire about it, to challenge it, to learn from it. And it is the actual voices, the actual images, and the actual materials of the past that enable my students to do so. Getting beyond all those who profess to tell them how to think about the past, my students determine how to think about the past for themselves.

References

Alcott, Louisa May. 1983 [1868]. *Little Women*. New York: Price Stern Sloan.

Atwell, Nancie. 1998. *In the Middle*. Portsmouth, NH: Heinemann.

Baum, Frank. 1960. *The Wonderful Wizard of Oz*. New York: Dover Publications.

Bjork, Christina. 1993. *The Other Alice: The Story of Alice Liddell and Alice in Wonderland*. Stockholm: Raben and Sjogren.

Bradford, William. 1898 [1856]. *Of Plymouth Plantation*. Boston: Wright and Potter.

Brown, Cynthia Stokes. 1994. *Connecting with the Past: History Workshop in Middle and High Schools*. Portsmouth, NH: Heinemann.

Burnett, Frances Hodgson. 1987 [1911]. *The Secret Garden*. New York: HarperCollins Juvenile Books.

Buzzeo, Toni, and Jane Kurtz. 1999. *Terrific Connections with Authors, Illustrators, and Storytellers: Real Space and Virtual Links*. Englewood, CO: Libraries Unlimited.

Cameron, Ann, adapter. 1995. *The Kidnapped Prince: The Life of Olaudah Equiano*. New York: Knopf.

Carroll, Lewis. 1866. *Alice's Adventures in Wonderland*. London: Macmillan.

———. 1966 [1890]. *The Nursery Alice*. New York, NY: Dover Publications.

———. 1985. *Alice's Adventures Underground*. London: Pavilion Books.

———. 1999. *Eight or Nine Wise Words about Letter-Writing*. Delray Beach, FL: Levenger Press.

Channing L. Bete Co., Inc. 1980. *About the Constitution of the United States of America: We the People*. South Deerfield, MA.

Cheever, George B., ed. 1848. *The Journal of The Pilgrims at Plymouth, in New England, in 1620: Reprinted from the Original Volume*. New York: John Wiley.

Ciseneros, Sandra. 1991. *The House on Mango Street*. New York: Vintage Books.

Collier, James Lincoln. 1989. *My Brother Sam Is Dead*. New York: Scholastic.

Curtis, Christopher Paul. 1997. *The Watson's Go To Birmingham—1963*.

Cushman, Karen. 1995. *Catherine, Called Birdy*. New York: HarperTrophy.

Dillard, Annie. 1996. *Mornings Like This: Found Poems*. New York: HarperPerennial.

Dorris, Michael. 1994. *Guests*. New York: Hyperion.

Edinger, Monica. 1995. *Fantasy Literature in the Elementary Classroom*. New York: Scholastic Professional Books. [Reissues in 2001 as *Digging Deep Into Literature*.]

Edinger, Monica, and Stephanie Fins. 1998. *Far Away and Long Ago: Young Historians in the Classroom*. York, ME: Stenhouse.

Egan, Kieran. 1990. *Imagination in Teaching and Learning: The Middle School Years*. Chicago: University of Chicago Press.

Equiano, Olaudah. 1995 [1789]. *The Interesting Narrative and Other Writings*. New York: Penguin Books.

Erdrich, Louise. 1999. *The Birchbark House*. New York: Hyperion.

Frank, Anne. 1955 [1947]. *The Diary of Anne Frank*. London: Pan Books.

———. 1995. *The Diary of a Young Girl: The Definitive Edition*. New York: Doubleday.

Forbes, Esther. 1943. *Johnny Tremain*. Boston: Houghton Mifflin.

Galt, Margot Fortunato. 1992. *The Story in History: Writing Your Way into the American Experience*. New York: Teachers & Writers Collaborative.

Gardner, Howard. 1985. *Frames of Mind*. New York: Basic Books.

———. 1991. *The Unschooled Mind: How Children Think and How Schools Should Teach*. New York: Basic Books.

———. 1999. *The Disciplined Mind: What All Students Should Understand*. New York: Basic Books.

Goleman, Daniel. 1995. *Emotional Intelligence*. New York: Bantam Books.

Gottlieb, L. (Producer), and J. M. Silver (Director). 1972. *The Immigrant Experience* [Videotape]. Los Angeles: Learning Company of America.

Graves, Donald H. 1983. *Writing: Teachers and Children at Work*. Portsmouth, NH: Heinemann.

Hansen, Joyce, and Gary McGowan. 1998. *Breaking Ground, Breaking Silence: The Story of New York's African American Burial Ground*. New York: Henry Holt.

Hesse, Karen. 1993. *Letters from Rifka*. New York: Puffin Books.

Hickey, M. Gail. 1999. *Bringing History Home: Local and Family History Projects for Grades K–6*. Boston: Allyn and Bacon.

Hirsch, E. D. 1987. *Cultural Literacy*. Boston: Houghton Mifflin.

Hughes, Monica. 1959. *My Naughty Little Sister*. London: Puffin Books.

Josse, Barbara M. 1995. *The Morning Chair*. New York: Clarion.

King, Casey, and Linda Barrett Osborne. 1997. *Oh, Freedom! Kids Talk About the Civil Right Movement with the People Who Made It Happen*. New York: Knopf.

Kobrin, David. 1996. *Beyond the Textbook: Teaching History Using Documents and Primary Sources*. Portsmouth, NH: Heinemann.

Kohn, Alfie. 1999. *The Schools Our Children Deserve*. Boston: Houghton Mifflin.

Kurtz, Jane. 1991. *Ethiopia: Roof of Africa*. New York: Dillon Press.

———. 1997. *Only a Pigeon*. New York: Simon and Schuster.

———. 1998. *The Storyteller's Beads*. San Diego: Harcourt Brace.

Lasky, Kathryn. 1996. *A Journey to the New World: The Diary of Remember Patience Whipple*. New York: Scholastic.

———. 1986. *The Night Journey*. New York: Viking.

Levine, Gail Carson. 1999. *Dave at Night*. New York: HarperCollins.

———. 1997. *Ella Enchanted*. New York: HarperCollins.

Lindquist, Tarry. 1997. *Ways That Work: Putting Social Studies Standards into Practice*. Portsmouth, NH: Heinemann.

Loewen, James W. 1999. *Lies Across America: What Our Historic Sites Get Wrong*. New York: The New Press.

London, Jack. 1982 [1903]. *Call of the Wild*. New York: Penguin.

Lord, Bette Bao. 1986. *In the Year of the Boar and Jackie Robinson*. New York: HarperTrophy.

Louie, Ai-Ling. 1982. *Yeh-Shen: A Cinderella Story from China*. New York: Philomel Books.

MacLeod, Anne Scott. 1998. "Writing Backward: Modern Models in Historical Fiction." *Horn Book* 74: 26–33.

Maestro, Betsy, and Giulio Maestro. 1987. *A More Perfect Union: The Story of the Constitution*. New York: Mulberry Books.

Meltzer, Milton. 1994. *Nonfiction for the Classroom*. New York: Teachers College Press.

Myers, Walter Dean. 1999. *At Her Majesty's Request: An African Princess in Victorian England*. New York: Scholastic Press.

National Council for the Social Studies. 1994. *Curriculum Standards for Social Studies: Expectations of Excellence*. Washington, D.C.: National Council for the Social Studies.

National Center for History in the Schools. 1996. *National Standards for History*. Los Angeles: University of California, National Center for History in the Schools.

Parkhurst, Helen. 1922. *Education on the Dalton Plan*. New York: Dutton.

Rogovin, Paula. 1998. *Classroom Interviews: A World of Learning*. Portsmouth, NH: Heinemann.

Siegelson, Kim L. 1999. *In the Time of the Drums*. New York: Hyperion Books.

Simon, Norma. 1997. *Looking Back at Wellfleet: A Children's Historical Walking Tour*. Wellfleet, MA: The Wellfleet Historical Society.

Sobel, David. 1998. *Mapmaking with Children: Sense of Place Education for the Elementary Years*. Portsmouth, NH: Heinemann.

Sorin, Gretchen Sullivan. 1988. *Present Meets Past: A Guide to Exploring Community History*. Cooperstown, NY: New York State Historical Association.

Spinelli, Jerry. 1990. *Maniac Magee: A Novel*. New York: Little Brown.

Stevenson, Robert Louis. 1948 [1886]. *Kidnapped*. New York: Grosset and Dunlap.

Tomlinson, Carol Ann. 1999. *The Differentiated Classroom: Responding to the Needs of All Learners*. Alexandria, VA: Association for Supervision and Curriculum Development.

Twain, Mark. 1996 [1885]. *The Adventures of Huckleberry Finn*. New York: Random House.

Watson, Edward B., and Edmund V. Gillon, Jr. 1976. *New York Then and Now: 83 Manhattan Sites Photographed in the Past and Present*. New York: Dover.

Weitzman, David. 1975. *My Backyard History Book*. Boston: Little Brown.

White. E. B. 1952. *Charlotte's Web*. New York: Harper.

White, E. B., and Peter F. Neumeyer. 1994. *The Annotated Charlotte's Web*. New York: HarperCollins.

Wilder, Laura Ingalls. 1953 [1932]. *Little House in the Big Woods*. New York: HarperCollins.

Wineberg, Sam. 1999. "Historical Thinking and Other Unnatural Acts." Phi Delta Kappa International, October 1999. <www.pdkintl.org/kappa/kwin9903.htm> February 19, 2000.

Winston, Linda. 1997. *Keepsakes: Using Family Stories in Elementary Classrooms*. Portsmouth, NH: Heinemann.

Zarnowski, Myra. 1998. Coming Out From Under the Spell of Stories: Critiquing Historical Narratives. *The New Advocate* 11: 345–56.

Zitkala-Sa, 1900. "Impressions of an Indian Childhood." *Atlantic Monthly* 85: 37–47.

Index

Trinidad: Stories of the Past, 133
Trouble, 129
Twain, Mark, 123

U
United States of America Quilt Project,
93, 95
University of Chicago Lab School, 55

V
Valley Forge (Pennsylvania), 31
Videos, as primary sources, 30
Virtual field trips, 55
Visual material, as primary sources,
29–30

W
Walking tour of lower Manhattan
(New York City), 46–50
Washington, D.C., 31
Washington, George (president, U.S.),
26, 98–99, 103
Washington Memorial (Washington,
D.C.), 29
Watsons Go to Birmingham—1963,
The, 109
Ways That Work: Putting Social Studies
Standards into Practice, 101
Wellfleet Historic Society
(Massachusetts), 44–45
Westfall, Alison, 68, 88

White, E. B., 26, 93
examining primary sources of, 11,
14, 37, 119
Whitman, Walt, 64
"Who's Who" of the school, 39
Wilder, Laura Ingalls, 125–26
Williamsburg, Colonial (Virginia), 31
"William Whytock," 79, 80
Windsor Castle (England), Royal
Archives at, 126
Winston, Linda, 39
Wizard of Oz, The, 119, 121
Wonderland Postage Stamp Case,
The, 122
Works of art, teaching goal of students
producing, 11–12
World Book Encyclopedia, 233
WPA Life Histories Collection, 68
Writers, teacher's goal of students
becoming skilled, 6–10
"Writing Backward: Modern Models in
Historical Fiction," 124
Writing process approach, 10

Y
Yeh-Shen, 120

Z
Zaire (Africa), 30
Zarnowski, Myra, 127
Zitkala-Sa, 126

About the *Seeking History* CD-ROM

The *Seeking History* CD-ROM is designed to help further your understanding of the teaching and learning that occurs when using primary sources in the classroom. It contains a wide range of student projects and voices, handouts to help get you started on your own projects, and links to primary source sites on the Internet. On both Windows and Macintosh computers, the program should launch automatically when the CD-ROM is placed in the CD drive. If it does not start automatically, simply open the CD-ROM and double-click the icon labeled "Start."